Bezalel:
Redeeming a Renegade Creation

CHRIST JOHN OTTO

Bezalel
Redeeming a Renegade Creation

Book 1 in the
THRONE IN THE EARTH SERIES
on the Arts, the Ark and the Word made Flesh.

Belonging
House

Bezalel: Redeeming a Renegade Creation

Book 1 in the Throne in the Earth Series on the Arts, the Ark, and the Word Made Flesh

Copyright © 2015 by Christ John Otto. All rights reserved.

Published by Belonging House Creative

Edited by Nancy Mari

Cover design by Lyn Silarski

Book design by Ed Tuttle

visit www.belonginghouse.org

Scripture quotations, unless otherwise noted, are from The Revised Standard Version of the Bible: Catholic Edition, copyright © 1965, 1966 the Division of Christian Education of the National Council of the Churches of Christ in the United States of America. Used by permission. All rights reserved.

Scripture quotations marked (NLT) are taken from the Holy Bible, New Living Translation, copyright © 1996, 2004, 2007, 2013 by Tyndale House Foundation. Used by permission of Tyndale House Publishers, Inc., Carol Stream, Illinois 60188. All rights reserved.

ISBN 978-0692615812

Dedicated to Dr. Brenda Meerdink
who taught me to keep 'em guessing.
Shalom.

Acknowledgements

A special thank you to those who have given me feedback and input in the beginning of this book series.

I am especially grateful to Rabbi David Fohrman and the AlephBeta Institute that helped springboard the ideas for this book. Special thanks to Michael and Zsiporah Moon, Bhari and James Long, and Christian Artists Together who all helped with feedback and opportunities to share this material and hone the message. Special thanks to our friend Ed Tuttle who stepped in to complete the book design. Ed also supplied an illustration of the Ark at the last minute. It has been a pleasure having him on the team.

I am grateful to Rick and Marybeth Holladay who gave me a week at the Art Factory. This was a challenging time that forced me to wrestle with this material and rework some of my presentation. Sometimes the things that do not work are the most helpful.

Thanks to Dr. Marilyn Weekes. Several friends suggested I write a series. Dr. Weekes suggested it in a way that I couldn't ignore.

As always I am grateful to the Belonging House family that supports this work, Jennie Fournier who heads up prayer, Lyn Silarski who adds a flair to every project, and the body of intercessors. Thank You.

Nancy Mari is the best. This is the second project you have edited. I know you will read this while you edit the book. Thank You.

Table of Contents

The Throne in the Earth Series.. XI

ONE   How to Approach the Bible and Theology 1

TWO   God is in the Details.. 13

THREE   Moses and the Call to Build a Throne for God 24

FOUR   Bezalel of the Tribe of Judah 30

FIVE   Bezalel Named by God.. 35

SIX   Bezalel Full of the Spirit of God.............................. 41

SEVEN   Bezalel Artist and Designer..................................... 46

EIGHT   Bezalel and the Beauty of Work 52

NINE   Bezalel Made the Ark 57

TEN   Bezalel the Priest 63

ELEVEN   Bezalel and the Messiah 67

TWELVE   The Mission of Bezalel.. 71

           Afterward 77

           Works Cited 78

The Throne in the Earth Series

There is a lot of tension in trying to honor the past while straining toward the future.

Culture shapers are called to create Renaissance. The word renaissance means "rebirth" or, more simply, being born again. In this moment in time, God is calling the church to be born again. And in order to do that, we need to go back to our roots, and our roots are before the last Renaissance and Reformation.

My Greek professor at Asbury Theological Seminary was Dr. Bob Lyons. Like all great teachers, he used his academic subject to teach about life. Whenever a difficult question was raised in class, he would say "C.I.E.": **Context Is Everything**.

"Context is Everything" is an important piece of this series.

In every age there are questions that get raised by people, nations, and cultures. **If you can determine what the question is, you can determine the correct answer.** The question being asked is the context for what happens afterward.

When I travel I share how I received the call to "raise up an army of artists who build Jesus a throne in the earth."

The first question is always "What is the throne in the earth?"

The throne of God in the earth is the place where God and Man interface. It is the place where heaven meets earth. Heaven is touching this created realm and making it holy. In doing so, there is a new order, and that order brings forth a new creation.

A Little House in Nazareth

Recently some friends gifted me with tickets to Israel. As I planned my trip, I had a strong sense from God that Nazareth was an important part of the journey. After arriving in Israel, I discovered that going to Nazareth from Jerusalem without a car was going to be quite an adventure. The trip required a day's journey by bus to Haifa and then another 2 hour bus trip to Nazareth across the valley of Megiddo and up the hills into the city.

In the middle of a bustling, dirty, largely Arab community sits the Basilica of the Annunciation. The current church was built in the late 1960s out of poured concrete. Already it is a structure that appears dated and out of place. Fortunately, in the past 2000 years a series of churches have stood on this spot. Hopefully this one will be replaced sometime in the future. I think the poor design is almost intentional, because the building is not why people come here. People come here to see what the basilica contains.

In the undercroft of this large church complex are the remains of a first century house. The house is part cave, part shopfront, part living space. Based on nearly 2000 year old graffiti inside the house we can guess who the original residents were, and from nearby archaeological digs, we know that there once was a neighborhood here, much like the one that's here today.

What sets this little house apart is the altar that has been built in its central room. Inscribed on the altar are these words:

VERBUM CARO HIC FACTUM EST

Literally translated: "The Word became flesh, *here*."

This humble house was the home of Mary and Joseph, and where they raised their son Jesus. Unlike many of the places one may visit in the

Holy Land, this one is a place of prayer, a place of reverence, and a place that seems to still carry the weight of the event that happened here. As Eugene Peterson put it in his paraphrase *The Message:* "God became a man and moved into the neighborhood."

Words aren't enough. We are seeing this every day as our world becomes more and more multi-sensory. The human race is dependent on the word becoming flesh. This is precisely why creative artists are so important at this moment in time.

God is in the process of creating a new humanity. God's plan was never to quietly reform human beings into a better behaved form of primate. God's plan was to recreate humanity into a restored created order that was actually better than intended in the first place.

God wants to create a new thing, not a reformed old thing. The plan is a complete renovation of this created order, and of the creatures who dwell in this place.

This is a series for artists and creative people, but it is also a series on theology and Biblical teaching. Although it might be helpful for preachers and others, these books are intended to help transform artists and creative people from the inside out.

Consider this: artists are the only people capable of having an inward encounter with God and then translating that encounter in ways other people can also experience. Music, visual art, film, dance, and sculpture all begin in the interior of an individual. Artists make the unseen real for others, and can cause others to encounter heaven's reality.

Only creative artists can make the word flesh.

Artists are uniquely positioned at this moment in time because of the unique gift of the artist. Creative people have the ability to have an internal experience—hopefully with God—and then communicate that experience to others in a way that they too can have an experience. All one has to do is go to an art gallery and you can see that many artists today are having demonic experiences, and they are more than happy to share their demons with others! At the same time, we can go back and look at the great masters and have our spirits lifted even beyond ourselves. Art is powerful.

Let me explain this a little more simply. Artists are translators. They translate the inner movements of their own souls into concrete forms that others may encounter. This is why so many artists are gripped with a fear of rejection, and would rather starve in a garret than risk showing their work to others. When a truly skilled artist creates, they expose themselves to others. The deepest thing we can experience in life is a spiritual encounter with God, and to translate that into art is a pretty risky undertaking.

From the beginning God has had a strategy. That strategy is taking the word and making it flesh. The process of making the word flesh is full of risk. We are going to look at some of the biggest risk takers in this series.

The Bible is like a tapestry.

In a tapestry there are many threads that come together to make an amazing picture. If you find a thread and follow its path, you start to see a theme that helps hold the story together.

The thread we are going to follow is the gold thread attached to the Ark of the Covenant. By following this thread, we will begin to see God's strategy for restoring his reign in the earth. We are going to explore how this strategy has been unfolding throughout salvation history up until now. We are going to first study Bezalel, the artist who was called to build the Ark, and how his life is a model for artists today. Bezalel was called out, filled with the Holy Spirit, and then he translated that inner experience into multi-sensory space others could experience. We are then going to see how the physical Ark, and what it represents, gets transformed in the New Covenant and how Mary risked everything to see the greatest expression of the Word made flesh. Next we will look at the Ark itself, and the role it played in the reign of David. We will also be looking at how the contents of the Ark—especially the Manna— becomes transformed in the life of Jesus to be a central aspect of the creative life. Finally we will look at the primary tool we are given to bring transformation: the tool of story.

We will begin this series by explaining some background regarding Biblical interpretation, the authority of Scripture, and the method that I use to "do" theology. I believe firmly that artists and creative people are poised to be the preachers and theologians of our era, and in order to do this, you need the tools to do your job well. The next chapter may seem a little technical, but it will be helpful as you read these books.

The LORD said to Moses, "See, I have called by name Bezalel the son of Uri, son of Hur, of the tribe of Judah: and I have filled him with the Spirit of God, with ability and intelligence, with knowledge and all craftsmanship, to devise artistic designs, to work in gold, silver, and bronze, in cutting stones for setting, and in carving wood, for work in every craft. And behold, I have appointed with him Oholiab, the son of Ahisamach, of the tribe of Dan; and I have given to all able men ability, that they may make all that I have commanded you: the tent of meeting, and the Ark of the testimony, and the mercy seat that is thereon, and all the furnishings of the tent, the table and its utensils, and the pure lampstand with all its utensils, and the altar of incense, and the altar of burnt offering with all its utensils, and the laver and its base, and the finely worked garments, the holy garments for Aaron the priest and the garments of his sons, for their service as priests, and the anointing oil and the fragrant incense for the holy place. According to all that I have commanded you they shall do."

How to Approach the Bible and Theology

Over the past year and a half I have been sharing a lot of the research for this book in small groups, with individuals, and with retreats in the United States, Europe, and the Middle East. Out of that experience I learned that the average person in my audience lacked two things: a knowledge of the Bible and how it is interpreted, and the ability to think theologically. Many of the people I meet (some of them ministry leaders) have grown so accustomed to pre-packaged teaching that they are spending little time in the Bible themselves, and less time in prayer.

Since one of the themes in this book is "risk" I am going to do something risky—tackle a boring topic right at the start. I believe that by giving you the tools to understand the Bible and theology, you will be like the man in the proverb who was taught to fish and so was able to catch fish for the rest of his life.

In this chapter I would like to give you the tools to better interpret the Bible, and also understand the "grid" I used to write this book. All artists and craftsmen need to learn their craft. This is essential to being a success. Interpreting the Bible and drawing good conclusions from the text is also a craft. I am going to attempt to distill about eight years of seminary into the next few pages.

Understanding the Bible

We need to begin with this tapestry, the Bible. The Bible is the greatest piece of World Literature that we human beings possess. It is the only book translated into every written language.[1] That fact alone should give you a moment of pause.

One of the most interesting things about the Bible is the fact it is first a work of art. It contains poetry, songs, a play, short stories and at least one story that is close to a novel. It contains parables, allegories, and it contains some of the most stunning descriptive language in all of literature. Ironically, the Christians who downplay the role of the artist look to a work of art to support their position. When you are involved in the performing arts you look for good material. We Christians have been given the best material of all.

Because the Bible contains so many different types of literature, it is important to recognize the genre when you are reading. In other words, you don't read a poem the same way you read the newspaper. Your interpretation and understanding of the text will improve when you start to read different parts of the Bible according to their genres.

Sadly most contemporary Christians do not know or understand the Bible. I make this bold statement based on observation—many of the Christians I know live lives or hold beliefs that are contrary to the Bible. They do not know where the Bible came from or what it contains. Many do not know how the various stories relate to one another. And many do not really know why the Bible has authority.

Many people miss the *story* because of a tendency to view the Bible as a rule book or a book of precepts and principles. Some read the Bible like *Aesop's Fables* and see it full of disconnected vignettes that each have a topical point or moral at the end. Others try to make the Bible support positions about science or politics. And still others enter into battles over inerrancy or infallibility.

---

1   I have had several friends who work for the Wycliffe Bible Translators. This is a group of linguists who are creating written forms of spoken languages and then translating the Bible after these tribal languages are recorded in a written form.

Trouble arises when we make the Bible say things about itself that it never said. The Bible never claims to have dropped out of heaven in a perfect state. It never claims to have been written by one infallible leader. It does not support any modern political or economic camp or system (in fact, it presents a clear alternative to all of them). The Bible is very different from other religious texts like the Quran or the Book of Mormon that make claims about all of these things. Surprisingly, final authority of the Bible never rests on individual authorship.[2]

Here's what St. Paul wrote to Timothy in about the year 60:

> *All Scripture is inspired by God and profitable for teaching, for reproof, for correction, and for training in righteousness, that the man of God may be complete, equipped for every good work. (II Timothy 3:16)*

This is what the Bible says about itself—it's inspired. This is why the Bible has authority—because God inspired it. And because it is inspired, people encounter God when they read it.

The Bible is an amazing piece of world literature. It has a 4000 year history. The writing and compiling of the Bible took over a thousand years. It contains stories, songs, laws, and letters. The whole canon—the 66 books acknowledged by all Christians plus the Apocrypha, and the Deuterocanon[3], have an amazing cohesiveness. As a work of literature the Bible has a beginning, middle, and end. It has a growing conflict that climaxes at the Cross and resolves in the Book of Revelation. All of the smaller pieces of the larger volume—the "books" as we call them—are stand alone works yet they all advance the larger narrative.

---

2   That said, the church has used apostolic authorship to decide what is allowed in the canon. Even here, there has been a blurry line. Hebrews and Revelation are both books whose authorship has been questioned from the earliest time.

3   Deuterocanon" literally means "second canon" and are the books that are regarded as Scripture by the various orthodox churches. Most Protestants only consider the 66 books of the Old and New Testament Scripture. Most Anglicans and all Roman Catholics include the books of the Apocrypha. The books of the Apocrypha are books included in the Greek Translation of the Hebrew Bible called the Septuagint, but have no Hebrew originals. Jews do not consider these Scripture.

A Father, a Bride, and a Son

For instance, the larger arc of the Biblical narrative (the "meta-narrative" to use scholarly jargon) is the story of a Father looking for a Bride for his Son. When you understand this, many things suddenly come together—the Bible begins and ends with a wedding. The middle of the Bible is this graphic book about a couple's wedding night. The first miracle of Jesus takes place at a wedding, and the major theme of the prophets is marital infidelity and sexual immorality. God's story is about a marriage, a family, and whole relationships.

And beyond the compiling, writing, and composing of the original material, the story of how we received this book is equally amazing. The fact that thousands of anonymous scribes, copyists, printers, and scholars have all had a hand in the transmission of this book and that it has come down to us remarkably intact should fill you with awe. In 1948 when the Dead Sea Scrolls were discovered, many were stunned at the accuracy of our modern texts compared to these two thousand year old fragments. There are thousands of manuscripts, and they give us a really clear picture of a book that has been passed on to us with very few alterations. When compared to other ancient texts, the Bible stands alone in volumes of copies, and the level of accurate comparisons.[4]

I believe every step of the process really was divinely inspired. Remember that even when there are puzzles and evidence of editing or changes in the Biblical text, **the process was still overshadowed by the Holy Spirit.** In this sense, the Bible is both human (it has a lot of fingerprints on it) and divine (God was the inspirer and master director of the whole process).

In order to find out about the Throne of God in the earth we are going to dig into the Bible and explore passages that have been ignored, suppressed, or overlooked. We are going to explore some apparent contradictions in Scripture, and the traditions of men that have arisen to cover them up. **In the end you will see that creative people are not at the fringe of God's plan for today, but in the center of it.**

---

4 F.J. A. Hort, *The New Testament in the Original Greek*, Vol.1, New York: Macmillan, p. 561.

Before we do this, we need to talk about how people have been studying and interpreting the Bible for the past 200 years.

Understanding Biblical Criticism

Tradition says that the first five books of the Bible were written by Moses. As I said earlier, it is dangerous to say things about the Bible that the Bible doesn't say about itself.

In the 19th Century a group of German scholars developed what became known as "Higher Criticism." They applied ideas from the Enlightenment to the Biblical text and analyzed it as a piece of literature. In this analysis they found evidence of various contributors. As I just mentioned, the Bible has a lot of fingerprints on it. These scholars focused on the human aspect of the Bible and ignored the Divine. Unfortunately, their study of the Bible was intended to undermine the authority of the Bible—and the church. Higher Criticism took aim at one part of the Bible in particular, the Torah. They set out to prove that Moses did not write these books. **They began from a place of disbelief rather than belief and depended on intellect rather than faith to draw their conclusions.**

The theory they developed said that the first five books of the Bible were created from four different streams of material, and that the four streams were organized into one book many centuries after the events happened. Because of this theory, which became known as "JEDP," many lost their faith in the authority of the Bible—and in turn, their faith in orthodox traditional Christianity.

Traditionalists, fundamentalists, and later many evangelicals took the opposite position, and emphasized that Moses was the author of the first five books. **They began from a place of belief and depended on faith rather than intellect to study and interpret the Bible.**

Although this sounds great, the "side-effect" to the evangelical position was the tendency to "turn off" the brain. Critical thinking when it comes to faith and the Bible has often been discouraged. This lack of critical thinking sometimes extends itself into the way many conservative Christians approach life in general. As a result many intelligent and creative people have dismissed traditional Christianity as a religion for ignorant people and have turned to revisionist forms of Christianity or non-Christian religions.

I believe that the truth is somewhere in between these two positions— Moses was probably behind organizing and composing a lot of the Torah, but there is evidence that others came later and edited the text. The Bible doesn't say Moses wrote these books, and that should not shake your faith in the Bible. God is the author. In other words, I believe in God's authority and I look at the Biblical evidence in the light of faith—and I also do not "turn off" my brain. In this book, I want to make you think.

This is important in our day because the tradition of Biblical interpretation that began with JEDP continues to this day. We see it in things like the Jesus Seminar that votes on which things Jesus really said in the Gospels, and the annual magazine articles about various books that "should" be in the Bible. We see it in cable documentaries that promote absurd theories about the Bible. We see it in "discoveries" of new gospels that the "Church" has forbidden. We also see it in various camps who choose to ignore passages that run counter to their personal views on sexuality, marriage, holiness, or charismatic spirituality. It is dangerous to take a knife and begin editing the bits you don't like. There really is no guarantee that others will stop where you think it's safe to stop. Eventually the editing ends with discarding the entire book.

The Canon

When we talk about the whole book, we are talking about the "canon" of Scripture. **The canon is the accepted content of the Bible handed down to us by the Church.** The canon gives us two things: an acceptable list of books proven to be inspired by God over time, and a boundary for continuing revelation. We have been given a gift that becomes a measuring line for all new teaching. *Newsweek* or *The Guardian* can come up with a new Gospel of Thomas or Judas, or Delilah for that matter, and it does nothing to shake our faith. The standard is set.

As I stated earlier, I believe the Bible was inspired by God, and that God spoke through all the Biblical writers. But, at the same time, all the

Biblical authors, including Moses, Paul and the Gospel writers, were gifted mortal men. Because of this, you can recognize that the Canon is like a mountain range—there are peaks and there are valleys. Paul can say that a passage is his opinion and not the Holy Spirit and that should not shake our faith. When you keep this in mind you will be amazed by the art and the craft we will discover as we dig into the Biblical text. **Remember the Bible is a work of art, and the authors were artists inspired by the Holy Spirit.**

It's an amazing masterpiece.

And in this masterpiece there is a mandate to build a place for God in the earth, a Throne as it were. This mandate has been there from the beginning. If you are an artist, this mandate involves you.

Doing Theology

So far you can see that I think the Bible has a lot of authority. But, how do we interpret it, or translate it into our daily lives? The process of making this translation is called "Theology." **Theology is something you do, not something you study.**

Albert Outler, a Methodist theologian, created a way to do theology that I believe is very effective. His method, called the "Quadrilateral," is the way I approach the Bible, and the way I approached writing this book. Outler came up with his method by studying the way John Wesley approached theology, and Wesley's process was based on his own background in the Anglican Church. By extension, this method has its roots in the Church Fathers.

"Quadrilateral" means four poles or points. The four points are Scripture, Tradition, Reason, and Experience. The four points are not equals, but rather more like filters that help us understand the Bible the best way possible.

The Scripture

In order to begin doing theology we need to begin with the Bible. The first question is always, "What does the Bible say?" This is why Bible study is so important, and why the canon is important. It is wise, especially with controversial subjects, to find out what the whole canon says.

In recent years it has become fashionable to make the argument "Jesus never mentioned _____." True, but Jesus said he came to fulfill the law and the prophets, not abolish them, and the law and the prophets speak a great deal about a lot of controversial subjects. In most cases the Bible as a whole will present a unified picture on a subject. This is also why it is important to observe the text and make note of what it says before jumping to an interpretation. And I always ask the question, "How does this fit into the larger narrative of Scripture?" Sometimes the narrative gives you the answer.

Tradition

Tradition often is a "dirty word" in protestant evangelical circles. In the next chapter I will talk about tradition in the negative sense. Right now lets talk about Tradition in the positive sense.

Tradition is the body of knowledge that has been handed down to us from our Fathers and Mothers in the faith. Tradition is our received wisdom, especially from the early church. Tradition is really our family history. It is the experience of the church interacting with the Holy Spirit and the Bible. Many are unaware that the Bible was not collected into one volume until the fifth century. That means that the Church was a going concern for a long time before everyone had a Bible. Because of this, decisions needed to be made by the larger Body of Christ. Just like when we look at the whole canon of Scripture we can get a clearer picture, when we look at the larger history of the Christian church we get a clear picture. For us today the early church can be very helpful. The Church Fathers, those who wrote in the first three centuries of Christianity, spoke clearly to a multicultural pagan society. It may surprise you that the very first extra-Biblical document, the Didache (c. 70 A.D.) makes clear statements about the hot-button issues of today—abortion and homosexuality.

Although some parts of the protestant community speak of the "Bible alone," it really is impossible to study the Bible without some larger framework of interpretation. Remember, Context Is Everything. By looking at and honoring the received wisdom of the Church, we can get a sense of how God has used the Bible in different ways throughout time. Tradition also prevents us from being bound by our own subjective interpretation of the Bible. Tradition forces us to submit our opinions to the larger community, a community tested by time and by a great cloud of witnesses.

Reason

After we review what the Bible says on a topic and see how the Church throughout time has interpreted the Bible, then we need to ask the question, "Does this interpretation make sense?" Is the interpretation reasonable, logical, and sensible? The Bible (and the God of the Bible) honors those who are willing to think, to process, and come to good conclusions. If there is a doctrine that seems foolish or nonsensical, then it probably isn't a Biblical doctrine. A lot of heresy and foolishness can be spotted through the test of reason.

This is generally where various cults fail. For instance, the "way of salvation" described in Mormonism does not follow logically, and requires suspending disbelief to the point where one has to give up their will to another person. It does not follow basic reason.

It is important to note that Reason is not equal with the Bible. The quadrilateral in this sense is a hierarchy: Bible first, Tradition second, reason third. John Wesley once said, "Humanity left to itself will reason itself to hell."

Experience

Finally, we have to ask the question, "Can this idea, interpretation, or doctrine be applied to my life in a practical way?" In other words, how does this change my life? Is it simply a theory that can be debated with no clear resolution? Is it a doctrine that cannot be played out in a person's life, but brings division wherever it is argued? Does this idea produce good fruit in people's lives?

All good theology is going to produce positive fruit. Good fruit looks like transformed lives, healed relationships, and growth.

Of course there is serious danger when you begin with your experience or the experience of others (negative or positive). There have been many shipwrecked lives when the process gets turned around—experience first, backed up by reason, then looking for the minority report in church history, and finally, doing "mental gymnastics" with the Bible. If you put the process of doing theology together this way, you are actually trying to push the limit on what the Bible says, rather than trying to honestly let the Bible speak to you. It is the difference between wholeheartedly staying behind a guardrail, and seeing how close to the edge of a cliff you can stand before falling off. Good theology is letting the Bible shape you. Bad theology is you finding an argument to support your position.

Charismatic Reality

However, Outler's Quadrilateral is incomplete. I don't believe we can do theology in our own strength. We need the help of the Holy Spirit. Although it is a dirty word in some circles, we need to approach the Bible with a "charismatic" attitude. I use this word because it is the word used in the New Testament. It means gifted and graced. We need the help of the Holy Spirit to connect the dots, and to make good interpretations. The Holy Spirit inspired the Bible, and He can help us understand it.

Smith Wigglesworth, the early Pentecostal evangelist, once said, "Some read the Bible in Hebrew, and some read the Bible in Greek, but I read the Bible in the Holy Spirit." I agree with Wigglesworth's sentiment, and when I read the Bible in Greek and Hebrew I ask the Holy Spirit to open my eyes to what's happening in the text. The entire process needs to be bathed in prayer, and even in a casual reading, the Bible is the gateway to a conversation between you and the Holy Spirit. Ultimately, theology is about a relationship with God, not an intellectual exercise. Because of the Holy Spirit's involvement, Bible study and theology can be dynamic activities.

In the next section, we will begin using these tools to explore the life of Bezalel, the master artist and the builder of the Ark. As we explore this man and his story, I believe the background in this chapter will help you digest some of the more challenging parts. There is a lot in the text that will help us understand who we are as men and women called to build a throne for God in the earth.

TWO

God Is in the Details

In the TV show *Monk*, detective Adrian Monk solved crimes because he had obsessive compulsive disorder. Each episode usually began by showing a crime being committed—so you knew who did it right from the beginning. Each episode of *Monk* was about how the mystery was solved, not the solution. What made *Monk* such a compelling program was how the writers took Monk's greatest weakness and made it his strength. His OCD caused him to never miss a detail, and those details solved the crime.

A little detail can make a big difference and color our understanding. When we overlook a detail, whether because we think it is not important, or because we think we know about the subject already, or simply because we are lazy, we can miss a big piece of the puzzle. Those missed details can cause us to miss God, because **God is in the details**. A little detail can make a big difference, and color our understanding.

The Traditions of Men

Remember in the last chapter I mentioned the negative side of tradition? There are many details that get overlooked because of the "traditions of men." These traditions are often the unexpected consequences of one person's attempt to fix a perceived contradiction or paradox. Others are just mistakes or decisions that were based on a need at a particular time. When Jesus spoke of the "traditions of men" he was speaking of extra laws and rules added to what God had directed the people of Israel in the law. Sometimes these traditions were simply interpretations of a text that became a law unto themselves—like the rules regarding keeping the Sabbath. **A tradition of man is any burden that places an obstacle between you and God.**[5]

Jesus put it best in Matthew 15:1-8:

> *Then Pharisees and scribes came to Jesus from Jerusalem and said, "Why do your disciples transgress the tradition of the elders? For they do not wash their hands when they eat." He answered them, "And why do you transgress the commandment of God for the sake of your tradition? For God commanded, 'Honor your father and your mother,' and, 'He who speaks evil of father or mother, let him surely die.' But you say, 'If any one tells his father or his mother, What you would have gained from me is given to God, he need not honor his father.' So, for the sake of your tradition, you have made void the word of God. You hypocrites! Well did Isaiah prophesy of you, when he said: 'This people honors me with their lips, but their heart is far from me; in vain do they worship me, teaching as doctrines the precepts of men.'"*

In L. Frank Baum's book *The Wizard of Oz*, Dorothy and her companions enter the Emerald City, and are immediately given a pair of green spectacles to wear. From that point on, everything in the city appeared green. At some point someone removes their spectacles to find that the whole city is white, and that the whole situation is a sham. This is really

---

5   This should not be confused with "Holy Tradition," the notion that practices from the early church are carried from one generation to another. This tradition has often been defined by the phrase from Valdimir Lossky: "Tradition is the life of the Holy Spirit in the Church." Lossky, *In the Image and Likeness of God*, St. Vladimir's Seminary Press, Crestwood, NY:1974, 152.

how the traditions of men function: they put a filter onto truth or reality, and this filter prevents us from seeing what's really going on.

One of the famous errors that became a tradition is a mistake St. Jerome made when he was translating the Bible into Latin. He confused the word for "shine" with the word for "horns" and translated that Moses came down the mountain with horns. This translation actually does make sense, because it makes more sense that Moses would cover up the horns on his head than cover up the light of glory coming from his face. Even so, this accident determined how Moses would be depicted visually both by Jews and Christians up to the 20th century. In art Moses is the fellow with horns.

Another "tradition of men" developed when John Wesley sent missionaries to America. He instructed them to have Communion "every Lord's Day," that is, weekly. These men were called circuit riders, and they spent most of their lives on horseback planting churches. Unfortunately, because the churches were far apart and there were few ordained clergy, most Methodist chapels celebrated Holy Communion once every three months, when the circuit rider was present. Those circumstances created a tradition in the Methodist church that continued up until the 1990s. Most American Methodist churches only had communion four times a year.

Some other examples of how the traditions of men can cause us to miss a detail include the ways Scripture is misquoted. Probably the greatest example is "money is the root of all evil." The text says "the love of money is the root of all evils.[6]" Another example is "that's just their cross to bear." The way that phrase is used has nothing to do with what Jesus described when he talked about taking up your cross and becoming a disciple.

There are also secular traditions that are promoted by the mass media. Adolph Hitler once said that "Any lie can become truth if it is repeated often enough." One of these lies is the statistic that half of all marriages end in divorce. The real marriage statistics indicate that even when the divorce numbers in the United States reached their highest in

---

6   I Timothy 6:10

the late 1970s, the actual numbers were nowhere near fifty percent. Even so, this false statistic persists.[7]

Punishment or Fellowship?

Sometimes we read the Bible and our minds have been so formed by established interpretations that we miss what is actually being said. For instance, many Christians have been so formed by the "penal substitution" interpretation of the cross that other themes in Scripture are missed. Because this filter is so prevalent, many read everything in the Bible in terms of sin, punishment, and forgiveness. When I ask a room full of people to explain to me about the Tabernacle in the Wilderness and the purpose of the Brazen Altar, immediately I am given descriptions of sin, punishment, and restitution.

Then I ask the audience, "Why does Leviticus require all the sacrifices to be salted?" *Silence.*

What was really going on in the Tabernacle? Because we have lost one of the central themes in Scripture, we have lost the connection with the central role of the Tabernacle: to eat and drink with God. The brazen altar was actually a portable barbecue grill, and the offerings were intended to be eaten—by the priests and the fellow worshipers. If you read Leviticus from a hospitality perspective, you suddenly see that the bigger sin required the bigger offering. The "punishment" was paying for another family's picnic. Even in the sacrificial system there was grace. And my guess is, if you sacrificed a bull, there were many who shared with you in the feast. The covering of your sin became the cause for someone else's celebration.

In fact, it is difficult to draw a direct plot line through Scripture if your primary metaphor is one based on the penal code, but it is very easy to see a plot line through Scripture if your primary metaphor is one of hospitality. Eating, drinking, welcoming the stranger, and even being in or outside of relationship is key to understanding the Bible.

---

7   "The Divorce Surge is Over, but the Myth Lives On." Clair Cain Miller, *The New York Times*, December 2, 2014. This is one article of many on the subject.

Look at all the encounters in the Bible based on eating and drinking: Abraham and the three strangers, Joseph and his brothers, the first encounter with God and the elders of Israel, Gideon and the Angel, Ruth and Boaz, Solomon and the Queen of Sheba, half of the ministry of Jesus, a third of the Book of Acts, and the end of the book of Revelation.

A tradition that began with reformation era lawyers has made it hard for us to see this central theme.

The Bible is about belonging. And if you begin to look at the Bible in these terms, suddenly God goes from being the frowning judge to the loving Father who wants to welcome his children home. But like a father who has difficult children, there is a hint of the broken heart in the corner of his eye. And like every loving Father, there are children who refuse to come home, and those children choose to be outside the family. The reality of hell is not about punishment, it's about broken relationships.

Throughout this book we are going to be looking at details. We are going to follow some themes that you may have overlooked or misunderstood.

Training the Eye to See

Although I have dabbled in all the arts, my primary professional and personal medium has been illustration and painting. Very early on all good drawing teachers tell their students that drawing is about learning how to see. If you can see the component structures and forms in an object, you can begin to accurately represent it in ink, pencil, or paint.

The traditions of men keep you from seeing the details. You will miss the details if you jump to interpreting without first making an honest observation. If you begin with the assumption you know what the text says or means you will not see the forms, structures and underlying threads in the tapestry that is the Bible. It takes serious discipline and humility to continually look at the Bible with fresh eyes. Unfortunately we all gloss over familiar bits or quickly interpret the verse before seeing what the text says.

We are now going to start looking at some of the details.

Remember, **God is in the details.**

There are many stories in the Bible that get repeated, and most of us who have spent a lot of time in church think we know them. One of those oft repeated stories is the beginning of Solomon's reign as king. If you are a Christian you know the story: the boy-king Solomon is in his room doing his morning devotions and God comes to him and offers him anything, and Solomon chooses wisdom. And because of this God tells Solomon "You won the jackpot!" and God gives Solomon a lot of other stuff too. The moral of the story—seek wisdom and you can have everything else you want as a bonus!

However—this isn't what the text says. Often the Bible is about the story, not the "moral of the story." Remember, the Bible is not like *Aesop's Fables*. We can't take random bits out of context, state a moral at the end, and be done with it. Sadly many Christians, even major leaders and teachers, do this all the time.

So back to the details and Solomon. Here is the **context** of that story:

> And Solomon, and all the assembly with him, went to the high place that was at Gibeon; for the tent of meeting of God, which Moses the servant of the LORD had made in the wilderness, was there. (But David had brought up the Ark of God from Kiriath-jearim to the place that David had prepared for it, for he had pitched a tent for it in Jerusalem.) Moreover the bronze altar that Bezalel the son of Uri, son of Hur, had made, was there before the tabernacle of the LORD. And Solomon and the assembly sought the LORD. And Solomon went up there to the bronze altar before the LORD, which was at the tent of meeting, and offered a thousand burnt offerings upon it. In that night God appeared to Solomon, and said to him, "Ask what I shall give you."
> —II Chronicles 1:3-7

So we have a lot of details that most believers do not even know (I didn't know some of them until I began writing this book).

- **There were two tents of worship**—the Tabernacle of Moses, and the Tabernacle of David.

- The Ark was not in the Tabernacle of Moses at the time of David.

- **Solomon was an adult, and he was not alone, but with a large entourage.** He and his entire court sacrificed a thousand offerings, and sought the Lord in the context of Sacrifice.

- **Finally, the text highlights that the bronze altar, made by Bezalel, the Son of Uri, the Grandson of Hur, was a key part of this event.** Solomon sought the Lord before this altar, not the Ark.

This last little detail is the one that begins our mystery story. Why were there two tents of worship? Who was Bezalel? What does his name mean? Why is he important to Solomon? Why is he highlighted here? We are going to answer some of these questions in a later book in this series. For now let's stick to Bezalel.

The Invisible Artist and Designer

Five and a half chapters of the Bible are dedicated to Bezalel and the intricate details of his work. That's 157 verses, but who's counting? For the record, Bezalel gets more space in the Bible than Noah (less than four chapters), Gideon (three chapters), Samson (less than three), and Ruth (four).

I am guessing you have never read a book about him.[8] You have never heard a sermon focused on him, but you may have heard him used as an illustration for a sermon about something unrelated to his call or work. I have heard him referred to as an architect, builder, and even recently a gifted administrator, but not called what the Hebrew calls him—artisan and designer.

He is the first person in the Bible who was "filled" with the Spirit of God. This is New Testament language. Yet even this distinction is minimized by scholars and overlooked, either because of theological prejudice against the "charismatic" or because the scholar is focused on other topics.

---

8 When I began writing this book, I began a quest to find another book on Bezalel. I can confidently say that at least in English there has been no in depth treatment of Bezalel.

When you head to a theological library, to commentaries, and to study Bibles, the notes about him are brief, or non-existent. Often the notes will say "see note on page 233 about Moses." This is amazing, since there are clear issues with the text that would normally raise the interest of Bible scholars. Bezalel is so overlooked that the most important scholarly text on the Old Testament, Walther Eichrodt's two-volume *Theology of the Old Testament* makes no reference to him (although in the index he does make reference to "berzerker," a weapon used by the Vikings). In my research I found another Old Testament theology entitled *God's Design*. Although the author used the theme of design as his driving idea, there was no mention of the only designer mentioned in Scripture.

Among the many characters in the Biblical story, Bezalel is unique. His uniqueness is not only in the job he was called to do (creating the first portable worship center for God on earth), but also in his experience with God, his unique calling by God, and the characteristics attributed to him. Along with this, he is the forefather of some of the most important people in the Bible. Bezalel has been hidden, and he has been hidden because he was an artist.

Why has Bezalel been overlooked? Why are so many artists overlooked? Maybe you have been hidden, overlooked, or passed over. Maybe you have had an amazing call by God to change the world. If that resonates with you, then read on; you may have a lot in common with Bezalel.

You may have heard of Bezalel. He is the most often used proof-text for evangelical Christian artists. An example of this approach is Eugene Veith's *The Gift of Art*. Veith uses Bezalel as a springboard for a larger discussion of Christians in the arts without exploring the Biblical record concerning Bezalel. Or you may have heard Bezalel mentioned by non-artists. Those references are generally in a generic study on the Holy Spirit. Bezalel first came to my attention in this way through the Holy Spirit Weekend on the Alpha Course.

In order to understand the Ark, and all that God intends to do in the earth, we need to spend some time exploring the man who made the Ark. Bezalel built the Tabernacle, but in order to do this, Bezalel had to *become* a Tabernacle. In this sense, he is the first person in the Bible to let the "Word become flesh."

Bezalel's altar is the first clue in an amazing mystery story. I believe that as this mystery unfolds, you will find that the call to be an artist is a call to be fully human. Bezalel is our model for the rebirth and renewal of humanity.

You cannot understand what God is about to do until you understand this man. And you cannot understand this man until you understand the larger context. Remember: context is everything.

THREE

Moses and the Call to Build a Throne for God

In order to understand Bezalel, we need to understand where he fits in the larger story. Bezalel is an important character in the larger drama of Exodus.

After the people of Israel were led to freedom by Moses, they began to set up camp in the wilderness and Moses ascended Mount Sinai. On that visit he received the first installment of the Law, including the Ten Commandments. After this initial meeting he came down from the mountain, declared the law he received and made a sacrifice. Then he did something that gets sanitized in religious pictures. He took basins of blood and sprinkled the people, and the altar with the blood. Then something really surprising happens.

> *Then Moses and Aaron, Nadab, and Abihu, and seventy of the elders of Israel went up, and they saw the God of Israel; and there was under his feet as it were a pavement of sapphire stone, like the very heaven for clearness. And he did not lay his hand on the chief men of the people of Israel; they beheld God, and ate and drank. —Exodus 24:9-11*

As you will see many times, context changes what we think we know about the Bible. Before Moses goes up onto the mountain for forty days and forty nights, he brings the entire leadership of Israel up on the mountain (covered in blood!) and they see God face to face and have a dinner party. Only after they eat together does God call Moses and Joshua up the mountain. Eating, drinking, and seeing God face to face is the goal. When the covenant with God begins in Exodus, it is intended to be a covenant that builds an open relationship between God and humanity.

There is an amazing sequence of events in Exodus 24 and 25. After dinner, Moses spends a week on the mountain. Moses spent six days in the cloud of glory, and then on the seventh day, the Sabbath, God appeared to Moses. Maybe it took Moses a week to get accustomed to the atmosphere of God's presence? On the Sabbath God begins giving Moses instructions. These instructions are about a place of worship. It will be a portable place of God's dominion on the earth. This is the first link between sacrifice, Sabbath, worship, and the arts.

The first instructions in Exodus 25 are about the offering for the Tabernacle. Immediately after this instruction is the direction that is important for our study. God gives Moses the first description of the Ark. As we will see, much of the text from Exodus 24 to Exodus 31 is a list of incredible details. The details begin with the description of the Ark.

> *They shall make an Ark of acacia wood; two cubits and a half shall be its length, a cubit and a half its breadth, and a cubit and a half its height. And you shall overlay it with pure gold, within and without shall you overlay it, and you shall make upon it a molding of gold round about. **And you shall cast four rings of gold for it and put them on its four feet, two rings on the one side of it, and two rings on the other side of it.** You shall make poles of acacia wood, and overlay them with gold. **And you shall put the poles into the rings on the sides of the Ark, to carry the Ark by them.** The poles shall remain in the rings of the Ark; they shall not be taken from it. —Exodus 25:10-15 (emphasis mine.)*

When you miss a detail, you may miss the purpose of an object or a story. There are two details in this description of the Ark that are important to help us understand its purpose and what it represents. The details are the rings, and where the poles should be attached.

As I said, God is in the details. What if I told you everything you knew about the Ark was wrong?

The text says the rings must be attached to the feet of the Ark, and the rings and the poles to carry the Ark must be attached to the Ark's sides. Even with this description, most artists have created a version of the Ark that shows the rings at the top of the Ark and the poles running across the "front." Figure 1 is a picture of the Ark from the emblem of the Bezalel School of Art and Design in Jerusalem:

Figure 1

This is a very traditional depiction of the Ark. And because of this depiction, we imagine that the Ark is carried long wise with priests on the front and the back much like we would carry a sick person on a stretcher. These artistic depictions are based on some practical considerations. First, to put the poles into the feet would make the Ark difficult to keep steady. The center of gravity is much too high for practical movement. Two priests would find it nearly impossible to keep the Ark from toppling over when they carried it. Of course, the poles on the short end would counteract this problem, but now you need four priests, because two can't carry it. Once again, not very efficient.

Add to this another part of the description of the Ark:

*Then you shall make a **mercy seat of pure gold**; two cubits
and a half shall be its length, and a cubit and a half its breadth.
And you shall make two cherubim of gold; of hammered
work shall you make them, on the two ends of the mercy
seat. Make one cherub on the one end, and one cherub on the
other end; of one piece with the mercy seat shall you make
the cherubim on its two ends. **The cherubim shall spread
out their wings above, overshadowing the mercy seat with
their wings, their faces one to another; toward the mercy
seat shall the faces of the cherubim be.** And you shall put the
mercy seat on the top of the Ark; and in the Ark you shall
put the testimony that I shall give you. —Exodus 25:17-21
(emphasis mine.)*

Before we go further, imagine poles attached to the feet of the Ark, at
the bottom of the chest. Now imagine those poles attached to the sides,
not the front and back, so that they protrude forward. Now imagine four
priests, the four who are necessary to carry a top-heavy box with golden
sculptures on top. Imagine those four priests standing on the outside of
the poles, facing each other, holding their poles with both hands to keep
it steady. And now imagine the two cherubim facing one another. Now
imagine those priests walking sideways, and stopping periodically to
worship. This box was not designed for efficient movement. Maybe it
was designed as something else.

It reminds me of another passage from the book of Isaiah:

*In the year that King Uzziah died I saw the Lord sitting upon
a throne, high and lifted up; and his train filled the temple.
Above him stood the seraphim; each had six wings: with two
he covered his face, and with two he covered his feet, and
with two he flew. And one called to another and said: "Holy,
holy, holy is the LORD of hosts; the whole earth is full of his
glory. —Isaiah 6:1-3*

Fortunately, another authority seems to think my interpretation of the
text is accurate. The Temple Institute in Jerusalem has been creating ob-

jects in preparation for the building of the Third Temple. They have gone to great lengths and done a lot of research to recreate objects from the Temple that have long been lost. Figure 2 is an illustration based on their design for the Ark.

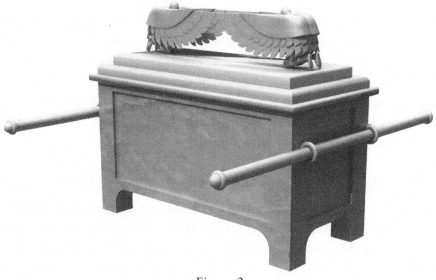

Figure 2

As you can see, the poles are still near the top of the chest, but they are attached to the sides and not the front.

Let me state at the outset that I know I am heading into dangerous territory based on my reading of the text. In doing research for this chapter, I discovered many heated online discussions—some even pointing to the movie *Indiana Jones and the Raiders of the Lost Ark* to prove their point! But please bear with me.

A Seat of Mercy

Martin Luther translated the word for the cover of the Ark "Gnadenstuhl." This means "seat of grace." His translation was influenced by the nuance in the Hebrew word for the cover, *kapporeh*, and the way that word was translated into Greek in the Septuagint, *hilasterion*. Both of these words indicate that this is a place where sins are "covered." It is the place where mercy, grace, and forgiveness are obtained. William Tyndale was one of the first translators of the Bible into English. He was influenced by Luther's translation. Although Tyndale did not literally translate the word from the Hebrew, he created a dynamic equivalent to the meaning. He translated it *mercy seat*.[9]

Imagine if the top of this chest, covered with gold, is really intended to be a seat. Imagine if the two cherubim were intended to always make you aware that the Presence of God was in this spot. Now imagine those four priests, all walking sideways and bowing whenever they moved that chest. Imagine that it was designed so no one ever turned their back to the Monarch. Also imagine if this was by design created to make the bearers move slowly, in tandem, in an unhurried way.

What if that chest, the Ark of the Covenant, was a throne?

The Ark is one of the most mysterious objects in human history, and it is clear from how it was described in Exodus and Leviticus that it was intended to be the focus of God's interaction with Israel. It is also clear that it resided in the center of the Tabernacle, and the Tabernacle was a model of the throne room of God in heaven that Moses encountered. If the Ark was a throne, then David's need for it to be in his capital city makes sense. If the Ark is a throne, it makes sense that the Israelites would take it into battle, going before them like a king. If the Ark is a throne, then it makes sense that it would lead them into the Promised Land, and be critical to the fall of Jericho. And if the Ark is a throne, we suddenly have an unbroken line from Moses to Jesus and into the New Covenant. The plan from the beginning was about the Kingdom of God. That Kingdom began to manifest when God held a dinner party for Moses and the elders of Israel—something that should have gotten them killed. They saw the face of God and lived. This Kingdom is all about the place of mercy.

The first direction that God gives Moses is to build him a throne, and that came right after he and the elders of Israel ate and drank in His Presence. Even here, in the beginnings of the nation of Israel we see that

---

9   Pelikan, Jaroslav, editor and Translator, Luther's Works: *Lectures on Titus, Philemon, and Hebrews* (St. Louis, 1968), p. 201.

God is about building a kingdom, and that kingdom is about creating a place of hospitality. God is asking Moses to make a throne that moves. It is not meant to sit in one place, and it is intended to be an extremely fine work of craftsmanship. Over the next few chapters in Exodus, Moses is given more and more details of this place for God. He is given descriptions of curtains, vessels, vestments, and furniture. He is given details about worship.

A throne is the seat of the reign of God. In a very real sense this object was intended to demonstrate the concept in the Lord's Prayer—Thy Kingdom come on earth as it is in heaven.

I can only imagine how overwhelmed Moses may have felt. He already has done the impossible by leading the people out of Egypt. Now his task has gotten worse—he now has to lead these slaves into freedom. But possibly worst of all, God is now instructing Moses to begin building and designing artistic designs. He's an old man, and until the previous few months, has spent most of his life tending sheep. I imagine if it weren't for the cloud of glory he was standing in, he may have been a little anxious. One of the beauties of the Torah is its honest portrayal of Moses. He is not the fearless leader. He is an insecure man who has great moments and really awful ones. The Torah shows us how this man "ticks" with all his contradictions. Moses was great because he saw God face to face and lived. I think in the end it says more about God than Moses. Moses is a great example of the point Kris Vallotton makes: "God uses broken people because that is the only kind available."

Fortunately for Moses, God always provides for the tasks that He calls us to. In Exodus 31 the Lord provides for the building of the Ark and the Tabernacle.

> The LORD said to Moses, "See, I have called by name Bezalel the son of Uri, son of Hur, of the tribe of Judah: and I have filled him with the Spirit of God, with ability and intelligence, with knowledge and all craftsmanship, to devise artistic designs, to work in gold, silver, and bronze, in cutting stones for setting, and in carving wood, for work in every craft.

And behold, I have appointed with him Oholiab, the son of Ahisamach, of the tribe of Dan; and I have given to all able men ability, that they may make all that I have commanded you: the tent of meeting, and the Ark of the testimony, and the mercy seat that is thereon, and all the furnishings of the tent, the table and its utensils, and the pure lampstand with all its utensils, and the altar of incense, and the altar of burnt offering with all its utensils, and the laver and its base, and the finely worked garments, the holy garments for Aaron the priest and the garments of his sons, for their service as priests, and the anointing oil and the fragrant incense for the holy place. According to all that I have commanded you they shall do." —*Exodus 31:1-11*

Here we have the context for one of the most amazing calls to ministry in Scripture. We are going to spend the next several chapters unpacking this call, and what it says about Bezalel, the reign of God on earth, and about us as creative people. From the beginning the arts, the artist, and the Ark would have a link.

FOUR

Bezalel of the Tribe of Judah

See, I have called by name Bezalel the son of Uri, son of Hur, of the tribe of Judah. —Exodus 31:2

God works through families. Actually, I think that God works through "tribes." Tribes are the largest extension of family relationships. The West is far removed from its tribal beginnings, and our society has been structured around the nuclear family. Because of this we miss the importance of the tribe in the Bible.

Some of my ancestors came to America in the 1630s. As a result, I have a lot of relatives. I meet distant cousins all the time who share my more famous relatives. These historical figures play an important part in the identity of my "tribe." Because of these shared family histories, I often discover an immediate connection to someone who only a few days before was a stranger. We are of the same "tribe." We share the same values of persistence and courage, and we really do have the same DNA.

From Family to Tribe to Nation

In Genesis chapter 11 the Bible begins to focus on Abraham and his descendants. Eventually the story becomes focused on Jacob. God would change his name to Israel. As the family of Jacob grew, he saw that he was no longer the Patriarch of a large family, but he was watching a family of families develop. Each family would become a tribe, and each tribe would become a nation. Humanity is hierarchical by nature, and that hierarchy comes from family through heredity, parents, birth order, and inheritance.

At the end of his life, Jacob blesses each of his sons. I believe he was acting as a prophet in this moment, and he speaks of the destinies of each tribe. Up to this point in the Bible we know that Judah is the repentant brother before Joseph. In Jacob's prophecy, we see Judah's role in the Joseph story was a foreshadowing of a future role. Jacob blesses him, and says:

> *Judah is a lion's whelp; from the prey, my son, you have gone up. He stooped down, he crouched as a lion, and as a lioness; who dares rouse him up? The scepter shall not depart from Judah, nor the ruler's staff from between his feet, until he comes to whom it belongs; and to him shall be the obedience of the peoples. Binding his foal to the vine and his ass's colt to the choice vine, he washes his garments in wine and his vesture in the blood of grapes; his eyes shall be red with wine, and his teeth white with milk. —Genesis 49:9-12*

An important idea in Biblical interpretation is "the law of first mentions." The first time an idea or theme is mentioned defines and interprets that idea throughout the rest of the Bible. This is the first prophetic word about the tribe of Judah. It is full of pictures that are echoed in the book of Isaiah, and also in the Gospels. They are pictures of Jesus coming into Jerusalem on a donkey, and of the Passion. **This is the earliest indication that the Messiah is eventually going to come from the tribe of Judah.** This is Bezalel's tribal context.

When Israel came out of Egypt, they were loaded with gold, precious materials, food, and herds of livestock. In Exodus 17 they suddenly find themselves ambushed by another nation, the Amalekites.

If the supernatural nature of Israel was unclear before, the battle with Amalek would make it clear. During the intense fighting the people of Israel would only prevail when Moses held up his arms. If Moses grew tired then Amalek would prevail.

To counter this, two men came forward and held up Moses' arms— Aaron and Hur.

Aaron is a logical person to be there with Moses. Aaron was the brother of Moses, he would eventually become the High Priest, he was a member of the tribe of Levi, and he served as Moses' "mouthpiece." Of course Aaron would help Moses, but who was *Hur*?

The Bible is a little murky about Hur, but we know for certain that he was of the tribe of Judah. It is hard to discern from the Biblical text if he was the father or the son of Caleb (I Chronicles 2:19), or if he was the son of Miriam or the son of a woman name Ephrath. Josephus and rabbinical tradition tell us that Miriam was the mother of Hur. Still others say that Hur was the husband of Miriam. Even the meaning of his name is elusive.

Even though there is mystery around him, the Bible is clear that Hur was present at the battle with Moses, not among the fighting force. In the midst of this crisis the arms of Moses were supported by Hur. Before Moses had even ascended the mountain after the covenant dinner, he had referred to Hur as one who, along with Aaron, could resolve issues or disputes. We can assume that he was in the inner circle of leadership.

We know that something special was happening in this family because Hur's close relative Caleb would be one of the faithful spies along with Joshua. And here is an important piece of information: **Caleb and Hur were of the tribe of Judah.**

I Chronicles 2:20 reiterates one more thing about Hur. Hur had a son named Uri, and Uri's son was named *Bezalel*.

Bezalel's grandfather held up the arms of Moses. It is probable that Caleb was Bezalel's great-grandfather. And the promise given to Judah in Genesis 49 was probably spoken over Bezalel, and he may have known this blessing by heart. Bezalel was a man of promise, and the larger context behind his work and calling is his tribe, the tribe of Judah.

We are now going to examine the call of Bezalel. His call is repeated twice, and it tells us a lot about this man.

> *The LORD said to Moses, "See, I have called by name*
> *Bezalel the son of Uri, son of Hur, of the tribe of Judah: and*
> *I have filled him with the Spirit of God, with ability and in-*
> *telligence, with knowledge and all craftsmanship, to devise*
> *artistic designs, to work in gold, silver, and bronze, in cutting*
> *stones for setting, and in carving wood, for work in every*
> *craft." —Exodus 31:1-5*

Called by name and by family

Bezalel is set apart by his father and grandfather, and by his tribe.

You have probably made the connection that if Bezalel is of the tribe of Judah, then he is a relative of David and he is also a relative of Solomon. And he is also a forefather of Jesus.

Remember that altar in the first chapter of II Chronicles? The one where Solomon went to seek wisdom? Did you remember an important detail in that chapter?

> *Moreover the bronze altar that Bezalel the son of Uri, son*
> *of Hur, had made, was there before the tabernacle of the*
> *LORD. —II Chronicles 1:3*

Although we may have forgotten Bezalel and his ministry, one of the members of his own tribe remembered and cherished the work that he did. A big part of this story is about honoring one's own history and heritage. Connecting with the past is important to our own stories and legacies.

Honoring your DNA

As I mentioned at the beginning of this chapter, I have a large family. One of my ancestors was a general at the Battle of Bunker Hill in the American Revolution. He is famous for saying "Don't shoot until you see the whites of their eyes." This story is passed down in our family, and every generation is taught about the bravery of our ancestor. Tribes are defined by their stories. **They are defined by the stories they share, and the values those stories represent.**

Caleb, Hur, and Bezalel are all early heroes of the tribe of Judah. There is no reason to doubt that David and Solomon were reminded of the steadfast example of Hur, the faith of Caleb, and the unique qualities of Bezalel. I can imagine David saying to Solomon, "See the bronze altar in the Tabernacle? That altar was made by our forefather Bezalel, a member of our tribe!" That story, and that DNA was in the mind of David and Solomon.

From our perspective Bezalel seems like a minor figure, but to David and Solomon Bezalel was probably a large figure. Your ancestors always seem larger than you. And David would have seen the work of Bezalel's hands on a regular basis. He engaged with the legacy of Bezalel, cleansed of the day to day details of his life. All that remains through time is the greatness. That greatness added to the greatness of his tribe.

Being a member of a tribe is core to knowing who you are and where you belong.

When we began doing ministry with artists and creative people nearly 10 years ago, I was looking for a name. I really wanted to call the ministry "Geborgenheit." My friend Ute Lahaie translates this German word as "the sense you get when you are being held in the loving arms of your mother." It is a place of safety, protection, and warmth. It is that ultimate place of belonging.

Being a member of a tribe is like that. You have people who understand you and connect with you at a deep level. They know who you are and they have deep understanding of your core values. Members of the same tribe "speak the same language." By the time of David we see that the tribe of Judah values faith, bravery, risk-taking, and having a heart of worship.

Many artists and creative people wander aimlessly without a tribe. Post-Enlightenment culture has succeeded in devaluing art and artists to the point where their only value is commercial. Much of the Protestant church has also succeeded in carrying out the values of the continental reformers. Even though many in the church are accepting the arts primarily out of a need to have cultural relevance, the underlying suspicion toward art and artists is still deep. As my friend Rick McKinniss has said, "The arts have been nothing more than an ox to draw the cart of evangelism."

Being a creative person in these two worlds has left me many times with the feeling that I belong nowhere. The arts community has become so dominated by the "post-modern" subculture that it is often hard for a Christian to find a place.

Bezalel's tribe is important because it gave him a place—he was a member of a tribe. That tribe was defined by his family, a group of people faithful to God and willing to take heroic risks.

As you reflect on Bezalel's life, it might be good to ask yourself the question: "Do I have a place where I belong?" If the answer is "no, " then there are a few steps you can take to begin to find that place.

1 Settle the issue with God. You will never find a place of belonging until you find a home in God's family, the ultimate Tribe. Do you have a relationship with God? As Paul said in Romans:

> For all who are led by the Spirit of God are sons of God. For you did not receive the spirit of slavery to fall back into fear, but you have received the spirit of sonship. When we cry, "Abba! Father!" it is the Spirit himself bearing witness with our spirit that we are children of God, and if children, then heirs, heirs of God and fellow heirs with Christ, provided we suffer with him in order that we may also be glorified with him. —Romans 8:14-17

Paul is using family language because you enter God's family through birth (See John chapter 3). When you are born into God's family, you suddenly find that you connect to others in his family in ways you never expected.

2 Look for like-minded people. Find one or two others who share your passion, share your values, or share your story. Get together in an informal way. I have found that coffee shops are awesome places to find and spend time with members of your tribe!

3 **Don't be afraid of relationships.** Creative people tend to be alone. We are easily hurt, and we can often be misunderstood. Stepping out into relationships is risky, but the long term rewards of stability, encouragement, and well-being are worth it.

In the next chapter we are going to explore Bezalel's name and the important thing it says about the calling to be little creator.

FIVE

Bezalel Named by God

The story of Bezalel's name begins in a surprising place. It begins before the beginning.

Before the beginning, there was God. Well, actually, there is God. Because God dwells outside of time, there is a reality before the beginning, and that reality is always *now*. Eternity is not a lot of time, it is *outside* of time.

Before the beginning there is God.

In other words, before the book of Genesis, there is God. We often forget that the Bible generally records events after they happened. The Bible is not the originator of the events. Genesis begins the story of this space and time reality. But there was a reality before the beginning. For our story, and for us to understand why artists have an important job to do, we have to get the perspective of heaven.

Heaven existed before this created reality.

Although it is true that this universe, and our planet earth, were created out of nothing, it is also true that there was something before this world. For that matter, there was something before us.

There was something before this created world and that something was God; and God's "world." We do not know much about that world in terms of a clear cut description, but we do know some things. We know that God is always in an unbroken harmonious relationship within the Godhead—Father, Son, and Holy Spirit. We know that this relationship is ultimately love—God is love (I John 4:8).

We also know that there are other beings who dwell in that world, and it has some history before our world was created. We have little hints in Scripture[10] about angels, fallen beings who were angels, and a realm beyond ours filled with fantastic creatures. This history, and those beings, all came long before this created order. Or rather, outside this order, because God's order is outside of time. All of this was before our beginning.

In God's heart there was a desire to have a relationship with a creature that would be like God. God wanted someone outside the Godhead, the Trinity, to love. And this desire to love and be loved is the preface to our story. The desire to love and be loved is where the Bible begins: In the beginning. It's a love story.

An Environment for Love

In the beginning of this story, God needed to create a place where these godlike beings could live. They needed a safe habitat where they could love and be loved, just like God. God knew that these new creatures would need things that the atmosphere of God could not provide. They would need a physical environment where they could explore and exercise influence. They would need a place where they could become and develop. They would need air, water, light, and food. They would need points of reference, time and space. They would need gravity, and they would need protection. They would need external things to provide order and balance so God created "interstellar space, the planets in their courses, and this fragile earth, our island home."[11] All of these things would reflect aspects of the realm where God lived.

---

10   See Isaiah 14:12-23, Genesis 6:2, and Job 1:6-12.

11   1979 Book of Common Prayer, Eucharistic Prayer C.

These ideas were first suggested to me in a talk by Rabbi David Fohrman of the AlephBeta Academy.[12] Rabbi Fohrman points out that this earth, this atmosphere, is like the womb. It is created to be a safe, perfect environment for the growth and development of a child. In the same way, this earth was a perfect environment for humanity.

Then after all the other pieces of this environment were in place, God created a man and a woman and gave them this command: "Be fruitful and multiply." They were to be like God, and become creators too. They were given this instruction: "Make little versions of yourselves that you can love, and that I can in turn also love."

And God saw this all, and God said it was very good. God knew it was very good because there would be more and more "little creators" who would share His infinite love. God also gave them the command to "subdue" the earth. It was to be their dominion, a place where they could exercise rulership as well as stewardship. It was theirs to enjoy, care for, and use.

B'Tzelem Elohim

Hebrew has a word for "little Creator": *b'tzelem Elohim*. Christians are probably more familiar with the Latin translation of this phrase, *Imago Dei*. The little creators are shadows of God himself. So from the beginning, the plan for this earth was to create little volitional beings (people who could freely make their own decisions, choices, and judgment calls) who would freely love God. These B'tzelem Elohim beings were the center of this new world, just like a new baby is the center of a young couple's world. God intended these beings to be like Him, and to rejoice in a world that was all about them—they would be the center, so that they in turn could focus their attention and love on God.

It is no mistake that before Copernicus the earth was depicted on charts as the center of the universe. From the perspective of the Bible, the earth is the center of the universe, and human beings are the center of His creation. **The earth was made for you, not the other way around.**

---

12 Fohrman, David, "What does it mean to be Be Tzelem Elokim?" Ten Minute Parsha video, *AlephBeta Academy*, alephbeta.org, 2014.

After He created humankind, God looked at them and said, "Ahh, very good, indeed."

Called Out by Name

In Exodus 31 God calls a man and tells Moses that this man will be given a very important job.

> The LORD said to Moses, "See, I have called by name Bezalel the son of Uri, son of Hur, of the tribe of Judah: and I have filled him with the Spirit of God, with ability and intelligence, with knowledge and all craftsmanship, to devise artistic designs, to work in gold, silver, and bronze, in cutting stones for setting, and in carving wood, for work in every craft." —Exodus 31:1-5

God called Bezalel by name.

Names are interesting things. I should know. Although my first name is very strange to Anglo-Americans, I was named for my great-grandfather on my dad's side, and my great-great grandfather on my mom's. To a German speaking family, "Christ" does not mean "Messiah," it means "Christian." Over the years I have grown accustomed to strangers coming up to me, misreading a list or a name tag and giving me a funny reaction. I have also gotten used to prophetic words from total strangers telling me that I am "anointed." That is, by the way, what "Christos" means. Although it is a challenge at times, I have come to enjoy my name and the heritage it represents. I think my name says something about me as a person.

Hebrew is a fascinating language. Every letter is a picture, and every picture can be composed to make a story, and these stories are words. So each word can say so much more than words do in English or Latin. And letters from several words can be put together with the roots of other words, and they can be combined and they can form names. Sometimes the combinations are simple and straightforward, like "Bethlehem." That is the combination of two words—house and bread. Therefore, Bethlehem means "the house of bread."

Sometimes these combinations are much more artful, and almost puzzling. At face value a word can mean one thing, but then upon further inspection, it means something much more profound. Added to this profundity is the deeply held notion in Hebrew thought that a name says something about the person who carries it. Names are important in the Biblical story. Every time a person receives a name change in the Bible it is a pivotal moment—so Abram becomes Abraham, Jacob becomes Israel, and Simon becomes Peter.

When God names you, you become a different person.

We can't really understand Bezalel the person until we dig into his name a little.

At face value, the name Bezalel means "in the shadow of God." Because most have considered Bezalel a minor figure, "Shadow of God" has been translated "protection of God," as in the first line of Psalm 91: "He who dwells in the shelter of the Most High, abides in the shadow of the Almighty." Few have taken the time to dig deeper into the meaning of the name.

As often is the case in Scripture a person is also named by their father. So in this case we can also translate his father's name, Uri, which means "light." It would be completely legitimate to translate the call of Bezalel, "See I have called the Shadow of God, the Son of Light." As you will see with Bezalel, he is like an archaeological dig full of treasure. And the beauty of Hebrew is in the digging.

The Jewish philosopher Philo, a contemporary of Paul, translated Bezalel into Greek. His Greek translation is *en skia Theou*. The word Philo chose for shadow, "skia" actually means "replica of." So instead of shadow in the sense of " in someone's shadow" Philo translated Bezalel to mean "a shadow of the original." In other words, Bezalel from this point of view would mean "a reflection of God."[13] Philo would go further and then link Bezalel to the concept of the "logos." We will revisit this later on.

---

13 Wolfson, HA., *Philo*, Cambridge, MA: Harvard University Press, 1948, vol. 1, p.253.

As I mentioned, there are many artful ways to unpack Hebrew words. Because of the pictorial aspect of the language, Hebrew lends itself to acronyms and acrostics like few other languages. Whole schools of Jewish thought and spirituality have arisen out of the arranging and rearranging of Hebrew words, names, and letters.

Rabbi David Fohrman interpreted Bezalel this way in one of his Parsha videos. His interpretation would forever color my understanding of Bezalel, and what he was called to do. Bezalel's name, at this deeper level, says more about artists than anything else. It puts Bezalel in the same category as the greatest prophets of the Bible. Bezalel may be the forerunner of all the forerunners in Scripture.

So what does Bezalel mean?

Bezalel is a conjunction of the roots of two other words: *B'tzelem Elohim*. As I mentioned earlier, those words appear in Genesis 1: 27, "So God created man in his own image, in the **Image of God** he created him, male and female he created them." (emphasis mine.)

The name Bezalel is an acrostic of the phrase we translate "Image of God."[14]

Rabbi Fohrman's view is supported by Philo's translation. Bezalel is the "little creator" we described earlier.[15]

Bezalel, the man named "Image of God" was an artist.

As I noted earlier, in the Bible a name generally says something about the person. Bezalel, the one called out to be the builder of a replica of heaven on earth, the skilled artisan and designer, is named the Image of God, the Son of light.

Since his name means the image of God, he is the prototype for all humanity. The call to build heaven on earth is core to being human. It is core to bearing the image of God.

Bezalel the artist is not just the model for artists, but the model for every human being.

14   Fohrman, 2014.

15   The acrostic is even more clear in the older spelling used in the King James Bible: Bezaleel.

And of course, by implication, the core to being human includes a lot of things: being filled with the Holy Spirit, taking physical territory and making it look like heaven, letting your creative gifts direct your work, and living a life of sacrifice. Creativity is core to being human. There is a lot in a name. Bezalel bears witness to the value system of the Kingdom. Being an artist, a designer, and creative person is the whole purpose for being alive.

God wants to give you a name.

For many years I struggled with my own call to be a creative artist. As a young person I heard the message that being an artist might be the lowest occupation a person could choose. And because I work with men and women who have struggled to walk into their calling, I know my experience was not unique. Maybe you have heard one of these phrases:

"Keep your day job."

"Haven't you heard of the starving artist?"

"But when are you going to get a real job?"

Maybe you have been "labeled." Some of the labels that artistic folks receive include:

lazy	reckless	critical
stupid	ADD/ADHD	egotistical
dreamer	irresponsible	

As we reflect on the power of the name Bezalel, the shadow of God, the Image of God, take some time to write down any names or labels that teachers, parents, pastors, or schoolmates have placed on you. You may need to forgive those people. Once you do this, ask God to give you the name He has spoken over you.

As you can see, there is a lot to this man Bezalel. In the next chapter we are going to explore the most important part of his life, and the reason he stands alone in the entire Hebrew Bible.

Six

Bezalel Full of the Spirit of God

See, I have called by name Bezalel the son of Uri, son of Hur, of the tribe of Judah: and I have filled him with the Spirit of God —Exodus 31:2,3

God works from the inside out and man works from the outside in. Few characters in the Bible reflect this truth more than Bezalel.

To non-artists (and that label can be safely applied to the majority of Biblical scholars), Bezalel is remembered for two things—building the Tabernacle, and being filled with the *Ruah Elohim*—the Spirit of God. There are no other details of his life, other than these two, recorded in Scripture. In this chapter we are going to unpack what the Bible is talking about when it says Bezalel was filled with the Spirit of God.

Outside In

Throughout the Old Testament most encounters with the Holy Spirit are clearly "outside in." Whenever the Spirit of God is mentioned, the encounter is basically a "boost" to perform a specific task. One of the prime examples in the Bible is Samson. In Judges 14:19 the "Spirit of the Lord came mightily upon him" and he decisively won a battle. In a similar way, when Saul was anointed king "the Spirit came mightily upon him" and he suddenly became one of the prophets (I Samuel 10:6). In both these cases it is clear that the outward anointing is temporary and the Spirit of the Lord eventually leaves. David must have also shared this experience because he pleads "take not thy Holy Spirit from me." (Psalm 51:11)

The Prophets looked forward to a day when the Holy Spirit is poured out and never departs.[16] This age is inaugurated when John the Baptist is told by God to look for the one on whom the Spirit rests and does not leave (John 1:33). This was the sign of the Messiah, the "anointed" one.

Inside Out

So let's take a look at Bezalel. The text says he was *filled*. There is a difference here between Bezalel and every other case before Jesus. And this distinction is what makes him unique. Bezalel is demonstrating a reality not available before the New Covenant.

The Hebrew word in Exodus translated "filled" is *mal-le*. And in this case, a lot is lost in translation. Both Hebrew and Greek have parts of speech that are non-existent in English. One word can indicate time, movement, or a state of being. The part of speech can be very important.

The word translated "filled" in the English text is in the Piel Imperfect Tense. This tense indicates that an event has happened in the past but in a vivid way also continues in the present and possibly into the future. It also indicates a change in condition. So to use this in a sentence "filled" does not mean "Gladys filled the birdbath," but rather, "the fountain began to run and filled the basin until it overflowed and it keeps on being filled." In this case it takes almost a sentence to understand a few Hebrew words. Paul uses the Greek equivalent to this word in Ephesians 5:18— be filled with the Spirit. The image used in Exodus to describe Bezalel is identical to the image that Jesus uses in John 7:37:

> *"He who believes in me, as the Scripture has said, out of his heart shall flow rivers of living water."*

Our English Bibles do not do justice to what happened to Bezalel. His condition was changed by the Spirit of God, and from that point on he

---

16   See Ezekiel 36:25-32, Ezekiel 37:1-14, Joel 2:28-29.

was a different person. Bezalel *becomes* a tabernacle so that he can *create* a Tabernacle. In this sense, because God is living in him, Bezalel really does become the "shadow" of God. And three times Exodus describes the dramatic creativity that he experiences. Bezalel receives ability, intelligence, knowledge, craftsmanship, and design skills. He also receives the skills of an engraver, goldsmith, sculptor, woodworker, and jeweler. And on top of it all, he is given the ability to teach!

Along with this bounty, Bezalel is given an assistant, Oholiab. Oholiab also gets filled later on, and his primary responsibility seems to be in the area of textile production and overseeing an army of weavers and seamstresses. [17]

With the power of the Holy Spirit comes the ability to create and manage a full-on production studio. What Bezalel would do in the desert falls somewhere between the studios of the Renaissance masters (really the only thing even close is the workshop of Leonardo da Vinci) and one of the big Hollywood art departments of the 1930s.

Although Bezalel has good raw material—he comes from a blessed family—the Bible is clear that his ability comes from the Spirit of God. His ability does not come from Moses, or Moses' authority. As Bezalel is transformed from the inside out, he does in fact become a reflection of God. He develops god-like qualities. As one commentator has noted: "Bezalel is given a level of creative capacity reserved for God alone in the rest of the Bible."[18]

At this point you may be thinking, "Big deal, it's just semantics." After doing a lot of research, I discovered that there are others who have tried to make a case that Bezalel's filling is simply another way of saying that the Spirit came upon him to do a temporary job. In this case it really

---

17   For simplicity I have chosen to not go into depth regarding Oholiab. His name means "House of the Father." In practical terms his contribution would have been enormous, but it is clear he is Bezalel's assistant, not his equal for several reasons: He comes from a lesser tribe (Dan), he is mentioned second in every reference, he is never mentioned alone, and he has a clearly different skill set, the soft arts.

18   Cassuto, Umberto, *A Commentary on the Book of Exodus [Hebrew]*, (Jerusalem: Magnes Press, 1952), p. 281.

matters, because Bezalel is called to do something unique in history—
Bezalel is called to build a replica of Heaven on earth. Take note of what
Jesus says in John 3:

> *Jesus replied, "I assure you, no one can enter the Kingdom of
> God without being born of water and the Spirit. Humans can
> reproduce only human life, but the Holy Spirit gives birth to
> spiritual life. So don't be surprised when I say, 'You must be
> born again.' The wind blows wherever it wants. Just as you
> can hear the wind but can't tell where it comes from or where
> it is going, so you can't explain how people are born of the
> Spirit."[19]*

It is vitally important that Bezalel, and his key helpers, be *filled* with
the Holy Spirit. God is calling Bezalel to give birth to a spiritual thing,
a thing that he has not seen himself. And it is vitally important for the
legitimacy of the worship of God in Israel that it not be a man-made
religion. The objects Bezalel creates need to be clear "shadows" of the
things in heaven.[20] Once again, Bezalel is a "little Creator" just like God.
He is the first person after Adam to receive the breath of God and begin
taking dominion—even if it is a very small piece of ground.

God is laying the foundation for worship of Himself, not just for
Moses or for Israel, but for all those of faith who come after. This unique
effort calls for a unique "anointing," so:

- **God calls Bezalel by name.**

- **God gives Bezalel his Spirit.**

- **God gives Bezalel his abilities.**

- **God gives Bezalel a revelatory ability to "see" what Moses saw on
  the mountain.**

Bezalel is going to create something that doesn't originate in his own

---

19 John 3:6-8, NLT.

20 See Hebrews 10:1. The earthly tent and its utensils are "shadows" of the New Covenant according to Hebrews, and Bezalel in creating them once again is a "shadow" of God.

imagination or creativity. His creativity is coming from God. Even the vision is not his, it came from a call by God. It is a God initiated, God ordained vision.

What sets Bezalel apart is this detail. His ability came from the Holy Spirit, from the inside out. Through it, millions of people would come to have encounters with God, have their sins forgiven, hear voices in the night calling them to great things, receive wisdom and anointing, and be fed. Spirit gives birth to spirit. In other words, it takes the Holy Spirit to create a supernatural work. Bezalel is going to bring heaven to earth, and be a supernatural being—a supernatural spirit-filled designer. He will become more than he could have imagined, and experience the indwelling empowering of God within.

Becoming like Bezalel

Fortunately, we are given the opportunity to have the same experience.

If Bezalel is the model for humanity, and for artists, then it follows that we too should be filled with the Holy Spirit. Not surprisingly, the New Testament makes the same case.

> *And do not get drunk with wine, for that is debauchery; **but be filled with the Spirit**, addressing one another in psalms and hymns and spiritual songs, singing and making melody to the Lord with all your heart, always and for everything giving thanks in the name of our Lord Jesus Christ to God the Father. —Ephesians 5:18-20*

> *Jesus said to them again, "Peace be with you. As the Father has sent me, even so I send you." And when he had said this, he breathed on them, and said to them, "**Receive the Holy Spirit**. —John 20:21-22*

> *While Apollos was at Corinth, Paul passed through the upper country and came to Ephesus. There he found some disciples. And he said to them, "**Did you receive the Holy Spirit when you believed?**" And they said, "No, we have*

*never even heard that there is a Holy Spirit." And he said,
"Into what then were you baptized?" They said, "Into John's
baptism." And Paul said, "John baptized with the baptism of
repentance, telling the people to believe in the one who was
to come after him, that is, Jesus." On hearing this, they were
baptized in the name of the Lord Jesus. And when Paul had
laid his hands upon them, the Holy Spirit came on them; and
they spoke with tongues and prophesied. —Acts 19:1-6*

When I travel and speak I encounter many like those who Paul met in
Ephesus, and I ask them, "Have you received the Holy Spirit when you
believed?" And like those believers, they too respond that they have never even heard of a Holy Spirit. The Holy Spirit is the Spirit of Jesus, and
without the indwelling Spirit, it is impossible to truly live as a Christian.
You are left with a "try harder" philosophy without the supernatural help
to succeed. Being a disciple of Jesus is impossible without supernatural
help. God would not ask you to set out in a boat and then take away your
oars. God has made it possible for you to be filled with the Holy Spirit.

**Bezalel accomplished all that he did because of God in him making
the impossible possible.** Unlike in the days of Bezalel, this gift is available
to us freely. He had to experience a sovereign encounter with God. We
simply need to ask God to come and fill us with the Holy Spirit, and walk
in that ongoing encounter.

Before his death in 1926, Cardinal Desiree Joseph Mercier gave this
advice, and I have found it a helpful way to experience the ongoing filling
of the Holy Spirit:

I am going to reveal to you the secret of sanctity and happiness.

*Every day for five minutes control your imagination and
close your eyes to the things of sense and your ears to all the
noises of the world, in order to enter into yourself. Then, in
the sanctity of your baptized soul (which is the temple of the
Holy Spirit), speak to that Divine Spirit, saying to Him:*

O Holy Spirit, beloved of my soul, I adore You.

Enlighten me, guide me, strengthen me, console me.
Tell me what I should do.
Give me your orders.
I promise to submit myself to all that You desire of me and accept all that You permit to happen to me. Let me only know Your Will.

If you do this, your life will flow along happily, serenely, and full of consolation, even in the midst of trials. Grace will be proportioned to the trial, giving you strength to carry it, and you will arrive at the Gate of Paradise laden with merit. This submission to the Holy Spirit is the secret of sanctity.

In the next chapter we will explore the work that the Holy Spirit empowered Bezalel to do.

SEVEN

Bezalel Artist and Designer

A few months ago I received an email advertisement describing an online course for church administrators. The advertisement contained a video. As I watched the video, I began to get angry. As the video unfolded, there was a voice-over describing the important work that God called Moses to do. According to this ministry, God filled a man with the Holy Spirit, and made him a gifted administrator for Moses. The man was named Bezalel!

There is a long tradition of misrepresenting Bezalel. Josephus, the Jewish historian who lived in the first century, went to great lengths to make Bezalel an architect without any supernatural gifting.

We began this book by describing how Bezalel has been largely overlooked by the Christian community. And sometimes when you look at different translations of the Bible, the picture of what Bezalel was actually gifted to do is not clear. There are a lot of words used to describe Bezalel's giftings. In this chapter I would like to unpack these words a little more clearly and settle the issue that Bezalel was a visual artist—not an architect, nor an administrator.

The Elephant in the Room

Two years ago I discovered a word that seemed to be intentionally mistranslated by Bible translators. It was the word for artisan. I later discovered from another leader in the arts that the word "imagination" was intentionally obscured as well, and only translated in a negative sense—as in the "vain imaginations of the hearts of men." There seems to be a blind spot when it comes to the arts. It doesn't help that often Hebrew can be translated multiple ways, and translators, almost as a rule, choose the least artistic reading in most cases. These experiences, and the misrepresentation of Bezalel raise another question we need to discuss.

Why do Protestants downplay the arts?

Once again, the answer to this question is context, and context is everything. We need to talk about the context of the Protestant Reformation.

Most Protestant Christians know that the Reformation was triggered when Martin Luther nailed 95 points of discussion to the church door of Wittenburg Castle on October 31, 1517. These points, called the 95 Theses, addressed the abuse of the sale of indulgences in Germany. To Luther's surprise, the 95 Theses "went viral" and suddenly a revolt erupted against the Roman Catholic Church.

Indulgences were certificates guaranteeing the pardon of sin in exchange for a cash payment. In 1507, the Roman Catholic Church began to build a new Saint Peter's Basilica. It would be a huge project, and by 1511, exhaust the Vatican Treasury. In 1513, four years before Luther's action, Pope Julius II issued the first edict granting indulgences for those giving to Saint Peter's. The next Pope, Pope Leo X would increase spending on Saint Peter's Basilica, and begin a full scale indulgence sales campaign. The money from this effort went to pay for the new St. Peter's Basilica, and for Pope Leo X's personal art projects. **Yes, I did say personal art projects.** "…Leo X's needs led to the worst abuses of indulgences and ultimately to Martin Luther and the Reformation."[21] These personal

---

21   Justice, Ginny, "The Role of Indulgences in the Building of New Saint Peter's Basilica" (2011). Masters of Liberal Studies Theses. Paper 7., 51. Ms. Justice's thesis is the first succinct work connecting the causes of the Reformation to the excesses of the Renaissance Popes. This paper is available online at http://scholarship.rollins.edu.

projects included works by some of the greatest of all Western artists including Michelangelo and Raphael.

When you look at St. Peter's Basilica, the Sistine Chapel Ceiling, and those two cute angels that Raphael painted, you are looking at art that was funded with indulgences. In addition, indulgences also funded the debauched lifestyles of some of the most corrupt popes. "With the enormous help of indulgences, New St. Peter's brought together the greatest visionaries, artists, and architects—possibly of all time..."[22]

Eventually the Reformation would trigger a series of wars, and the arts became the battle flag for both sides. The Protestants burned works of art and white washed churches to the glory of God, and the Catholics commissioned Baroque churches and monumental statues to the glory of God. Because the Bible became the primary interest of the Protestants, Biblical scholarship would become dominated by the Protestant worldview.

We cannot undo history, but we can understand why Protestant Bible scholars have continued to obscure the references to art, artists, imagination, and creativity in the Bible. Because these scholars have had such a huge impact on preachers, teachers, and church life in general, it is no surprise that artists would "go down the memory hole" and disappear. A distrust of the arts is in the DNA of the Protestant movement.

Back to Bezalel

Bezalel's call is repeated twice in the Book of Exodus. Four chapters of this book have discussed parts of the call of Bezalel in chapter 31. This call is repeated again and expanded in Exodus 35.

> *See, the LORD has called by name Bezalel the son of Uri, son of Hur, of the tribe of Judah; and he has filled him with the Spirit of God, with ability, with intelligence, with knowledge, and with all craftsmanship, to devise artistic designs, to work in gold and silver and bronze, in cutting stones for setting, and in carving wood, for work in every skilled craft. And he has inspired him to teach... —Exodus 35:30-34a*

22 Justice, 65.

We are going to look at all of these words and how they describe of Bezalel's work, and how they describe the level of his artistic gifting. In Exodus 35 there are seventeen distinct skills that are described. As I mentioned earlier, often Hebrew words have multiple nuanced meanings. As a general rule translators tend to choose the least artistic meaning when translating Bezalel's skills. Because of this Bezalel seems a lot less gifted in English than he is in Hebrew!

Intellectual Strength

The first four skills are what one would expect: ability, intelligence, knowledge and craftsmanship.[23] The first three are translated pretty accurately. "Ability" is sometimes translated "wisdom," and the Greek Septuagint translates it this way. Basically, the Holy Spirit is going to give Bezalel the intellectual "stuff" he needs to do the work God has called him to do. He is going to be supernaturally smart.

But then, right below the surface, there is a surprise, and that surprise is in the word "craftsmanship." The Hebrew word is "melakah." It will be repeated several times in this passage and it relates to keeping a business or operation running. In other words God is going to give Bezalel the gift of "business sense." It's the gift of oversight and leadership. In this sense, Bezalel was empowered by the Holy Spirit to be like the Renaissance Master craftsman. Bezalel will be running a studio. Just like today, being a gifted artist often requires a gift for business.

Sculpting and Carving

The next five words are a little surprising. Bezalel is given a handful of skills that refer to sculpture—not only in metals, but stone, and wood. In fact, one of the words, *charoseth*, made it into the modern Passover Seder. It refers to the stone work made by the Israelites when they were slaves. Bezalel will be given the ability to be a stone cutter, engraver, woodcarver, gold and silversmith, and to sculpt. It should surprise you that Bezalel is gifted to do something that seems to be forbidden in the Ten Commandments. He is given the skills to make three dimensional

---

23   I am indebted to bluriletterbible.org for help with these word studies.

objects that represent things in heaven and on earth.

You may remember that the cherubim on the Ark are to be made of "hammered gold" not cast gold. They were to be one of a kind objects, not something that could be easily reproduced, like the golden calves that were cast in pairs. As I noted in the last chapter, God provides a way for his commandments to be fulfilled. Bezalel receives the gift to make objects that are hammered rather than cast.

Makers

God is in the details, and the details expand in Exodus 35:35:

> *He has filled them with ability to do every sort of work done by a craftsman or by a designer or by an embroiderer in blue and purple and scarlet stuff and fine twined linen, or by a weaver—by any sort of workman or skilled designer.*

This verse contains the first reference to the Hebrew word *charash* in the Bible; in this version it is translated "craftsman." This word appears 35 times in the Old Testament. Really, the best modern equivalent is "artisan."

> *The artisan is a renaissance person, able to do many things and create things of beauty. In the books of Kings and Chronicles, this term would be used to describe the men sent by Hiram to build the Temple (I Chronicles 14:1). These artisans do all kinds of work, just like Oholiab and Bezalel—carving, carpentry, stonecutting, weaving, jewel work, gold and silversmithing, and design. The Charashim are the artisans/craftsmen called to all kinds of workmanship.*[24]

And even beyond artisan, Bezalel and Oholiab are given the role of "makers." They are called to make things and create things. This is the core of the word *charash*.[25]

---

24   Otto, Christ John, *An Army Arising: Why Artists are on the Frontline of the Next Move of God*, Boston: Belonging House Creative, 2014, 14.

25   For a complete study read "A Secret Weapon" in *An Army Arising*.

Designer

The word translated "designer" in verse 35 is *chashab*. It appears 134 times in the Hebrew Scriptures. It can be translated devised, designed, reckoned, and imagined. It's the same word used when Abraham believes God and God accounted him righteous. The gift of designer is the ability to see the unseen and make it real.

Colorist

The next word is translated "embroiderer" but the Hebrew word literally means "to work in colors." In this context the colors are brilliantly died Egyptian red, purple, and blue threads. Beyond being able to embroider, you get the sense that the craftsmen will be able to combine colors, understand how they relate, and use them effectively to brilliant effect. It also communicates the ability to use dye effectively to make colored material.

Textiles

Finally added to the mix is the ability to become a master weaver. I never understood all that went into weaving until I observed my friend Laura Savage plan and execute a group of weaving projects. The level of skill needed to create and execute a series of tapestries to become the Holy of Holies would have been a miracle of ancient craftsmanship.

Teacher

In the midst of this abundance of human endowment, Bezalel is given the ability to teach. God would teach him, and he would pass his skills and knowledge onto others. This capability would create a literal army of artists in the desert who would make and create a place for God in the earth—the Tabernacle. Because of this, the giftings were not for Bezalel and his legacy alone, but for the transformation of a people through creative gifting. Skills die with the skillful, but the skills of a teacher live on from generation to generation.

Life Abundant

Throughout human history there aren't many people like Bezalel. The word we use for a person like Bezalel is polymath. A polymath is a creative genius who can do almost anything. Polymaths are few. Possibly the most famous one in history was Leonardo da Vinci, who excelled in art, science, music, architecture, and literature. Some others you may know are Michelangelo, Hildegard von Bingen, Benjamin Franklin and Sir Isaac Newton.

What impresses me about Bezalel is God's ridiculous generosity. God breathed on Bezalel and created a multi-dimensional gift set that was used to make a replica of heaven on earth. God pours on Bezalel the ability to do anything. Most shocking of all, it's for art. It's for beauty. It's to make a place for worship. From a secular, human-centered point of view, it was a completely wasteful enterprise. It reminds me of another moment.

> *There they made him a supper; Martha served, and Lazarus was one of those at table with him. Mary took a pound of costly ointment of pure nard and anointed the feet of Jesus and wiped his feet with her hair; and the house was filled with the fragrance of the ointment. —John 12:2,3*

God lavished on Bezalel an abundance of creativity. And although the Tabernacle would be dedicated to God, the Tabernacle was for the benefit of the people.

I meet many smart, creative people who believe that Christianity and the Bible have nothing to offer them. Their perspective may have arisen because all the light, color, imagination, and beauty have been scrubbed from the translation. Due to this many think the Bible doesn't speak to artists or creative people. Bezalel is a witness to the truth spoken of in Psalm 87:7 "The singers and the dancers will say, All my fresh springs are in you."

It seems that the more gifted and truly talented you are, the more difficult life seems. As Luke 12:48 says, "to whom much is given, much is required."

You may be a person who has multiple giftings in music, writing, art, and movement. As we have seen, the Bible has a place for sculptors, those who work with color, those who work in wood and textiles, and those who make beautiful things.

There is a place for you in God's economy if you are creative. You too are a little creator.

As I mentioned in the early part of this chapter, being an artist comes with a lot of baggage. Many well meaning Christians have told gifted artists to give up their dreams to get a "real job." The best way to kill a creative person is to prevent them from creating. Bezalel's story is just an interesting Bible study unless it impacts your life. Maybe this is a good time to stop and pray about the things we have learned.

> *Heavenly Father, thank you that you called Bezalel, the Image of God, the little creator, to be a witness to us that you call and empower creative people. We acknowledge that throughout history art and artists have been overlooked and mistrusted by well meaning Christians. We forgive those who used the arts to define the battle lines in the Protestant Reformation. I forgive anyone who attempted to keep me from knowing and embracing the truth that You do call and anoint artists to build a place for You in the earth.*
>
> *Lord, release me from any mindset or belief system that tells me there are other more valuable ways to make a living, spend my time, or live out my life. Thank you for gifting me and I ask you now to release every gift and ability that has been "locked up" due to my false beliefs. All this we ask in the name of Jesus. Amen.*

In the next section of the book we are going to explore the work that Bezalel did, his most important achievements, and how that impacted his relationship with Moses.

EIGHT

Bezalel and the Beauty of Work

God is in the details.

In the story of Bezalel, there is no truer statement. God is in the work he accomplished.

As I mentioned at the beginning of this book, Bezalel is the central figure in about five and a half chapters in the Bible. Most of those chapters read like this verse in Exodus chapter 36:

> *The frames for the tabernacle he made thus: twenty frames for the south side; and he made forty bases of silver under the twenty frames, two bases under one frame for its two tenons, and two bases under another frame for its two tenons. (Exodus 36:23,24)*

Honestly, much of it is pretty boring. It's full of intricate details. Much of it is similar to Exodus 24 when Moses received the instructions to build the Tabernacle. Because of this, many commentators refer the reader to those chapters, and the notes for those passages.

So far we have learned that Bezalel received a dramatic and unique anointing from the Holy Spirit. Out of that anointing, Bezalel receives a unique bundle of seventeen different skills and abilities. And because the Holy Spirit is in the work, the work itself is sacred.

In order to understand this more, let's look at the context, again.

Spoiling the Egyptians

The job that Bezalel and his team were called to do was an immense undertaking. It would require an epic amount of raw materials. Those raw materials came from Egypt, on the night of the first Passover.

> *And Pharaoh rose up in the night, he, and all his servants, and all the Egyptians; and there was a great cry in Egypt, for there was not a house where one was not dead. And he summoned Moses and Aaron by night, and said, "Rise up, go forth from among my people, both you and the people of Israel; and go, serve the LORD, as you have said. Take your flocks and your herds, as you have said, and be gone; and bless me also!" And the Egyptians were urgent with the people, to send them out of the land in haste; for they said, "We are all dead men." So the people took their dough before it was leavened, their kneading bowls being bound up in their mantles on their shoulders.* **The people of Israel had also done as Moses told them, for they had asked of the Egyptians jewelry of silver and of gold, and clothing; and the LORD had given the people favor in the sight of the Egyptians, so that they let them have what they asked. Thus they despoiled the Egyptians.** *—Exodus 12:30-36 {emphasis mine)*

Israel left Egypt when it was the most powerful and richest nation on earth. The riches found in the Tomb of King Tut would have been only a portion of what the Egyptians, in a moment of national trauma, would have given the Israelites.

Think about it. Every caste in Egyptian society experienced the death of their first born son. That means the priests who prepared Pharaoh's tombs, the scribes who recorded papyrus scrolls, and the noble women all gave up precious objects. This includes all the luxuries of the ancient world—alabaster, precious woods, incense, and some of the finest weaving ever created.

These were the spoils of war, received out of the sudden shock and horror that millions of men and boys were suddenly dead. Israel survived this because each home was protected by the blood of a lamb.

Bezalel's work cannot be fully understood until you grasp that the beauty of the work came from the power of sacrifice. **The first Passover sacrifice was the source of all his raw materials.**

Offering of the Heart

Those raw materials get transferred from the people to Bezalel and Oholiab in the beginning of Exodus 35. Moses calls the people to make an offering, and they are greatly moved. Most of the chapter is an amazing list of jewels, brooches, precious metals, wool, and skins. We get a description of women spinning linen and preparing fiber. And we get a surprising list of luxury items that must have come from the Egyptian temples—incense, perfume, and anointing oil.

> *So they came, both men and women; all who were of a willing heart brought brooches and earrings and signet rings and armlets, all sorts of gold objects, every man dedicating an offering of gold to the LORD. And every man with whom was found blue or purple or scarlet stuff or fine linen or goats' hair or tanned rams' skins or goatskins, brought them. Every one who could make an offering of silver or bronze brought it as the LORD's offering; and every man with whom was found acacia wood of any use in the work, brought it. And all women who had ability spun with their hands, and brought what they had spun in blue and purple and scarlet stuff and fine twined linen; all the women whose hearts were moved with ability spun the goats' hair. And the leaders brought onyx stones and stones to be set, for the ephod and for the breastpiece, and spices and oil for the light, and for the anointing oil, and for the fragrant incense. —Exodus 35:22-28*

Of course, Bezalel needed more than supplies. Bezalel needed help. He needed an able, teachable army who could carry out the actual construction of the Sanctuary. The text records that a volunteer force also presented themselves as "a living sacrifice" so that Bezalel could complete the project.

The offering sets the stage for one of the most precious scenes in all of the Bible.

> *And Moses called Bezalel and Oholiab and every able man in whose mind the LORD had put ability, every one whose heart stirred him up to come to do the work; and they received from Moses all the freewill offering which the people of Israel had brought for doing the work on the sanctuary. They still kept bringing him freewill offerings every morning, so that all the able men who were doing every sort of task on the sanctuary came, each from the task that he was doing, and said to Moses, "The people bring much more than enough for doing the work which the LORD has commanded us to do." So Moses gave command, and word was proclaimed throughout the camp, "Let neither man nor woman do anything more for the offering for the sanctuary." So the people were restrained from bringing; for the stuff they had was sufficient to do all the work, and more. —Exodus 36:2-7*

I am guessing that free will offerings may have even continued after this offering ceased. The workforce would have needed food and provision, and it would seem likely that the people continued to bring food to help the project.

The first authorized sacrifice that Israel offered after the Passover was the one that provided the art materials for the construction of the Tabernacle. Against this backdrop of joyous sacrifice, the work begins.

Holy Labor

The description of the actual work starts in Exodus 36:10 with a reference to "he" and the "he" in question is probably Bezalel. For the rest of the chapter we will encounter a lot of painstaking detail.

Why does the text include this information?

Some commentators believe that this was included to guarantee that Bezalel was faithful to the instructions given to Moses. This is a reasonable, straightforward interpretation.

I think the purpose is more profound. Here we see a man who is being taught by the Holy Spirit. He makes objects that will form a replica of God's dwelling place in heaven. The work doesn't begin with the main objects of worship, it begins with curtains and curtain rings. The curtains are the boundary between the camp and the area reserved for worship and celebration on the Sabbath and Holy Days. The work begins by setting the sacred space apart, and by making a place in this fallen world holy. This seems like mundane stuff, but as the work develops, so the importance of the work increases. Bezalel and his team are growing, and as they grow, the objects they create grow in importance.

The Bible records the work of God through Bezalel, and that work is of value in and of itself. God is blurring the line between prayer and work, the sacred and the secular. All the world is called to be a place for God modeled on this microcosm called the Tabernacle. By implication, all the work on the Tabernacle is as holy as the Tabernacle itself.

I can't imagine being an artist who has been supplied with so much gold that it got into my hair and under my fingernails. There was so much gold that it could have been used to discover the unique properties of gold under heat, pressure, and force. And yet, in all this abundance, there was the ever constant reminder of the sacrifice: the sacrifice of the Passover lamb, the sacrifice of the Egyptians, and the abundant sacrifice of the people for the Tabernacle. The whole process from the materials to the end product was holy. The Tabernacle didn't become holy, it was holy.

The Bible is telling us that the work itself—the process of doing the art—is also holy.

If you do an internet search for a picture of the Tabernacle you will get a lot of results. Because of the rich symbolism in the structure itself there are many detailed drawings, diagrams, schematics, and miniature replicas out there. (The same goes for the Temple of Solomon, based on the Tabernacle.) There is one important detail missing from these representations. Usually there are no people.

Because the work was set apart for God's purpose so were the men and women who did the work. They had as much value as the Tabernacle itself. In other words, God doesn't discard people who do great things for him. Bezalel is a reminder to us that no one is expendable for someone else's vision. Bezalel now physically embodies his spiritual indwelling. Through his work he is becoming a sacrament, and every action he makes is worthy of recording. To the writer of Exodus, Bezalel echoes Genesis. He is the little creator of a New Creation.

The Bible's descriptions of Bezalel's work should validate and encourage those who work with their hands and make things. The Bible is giving us a picture of the spiritual life. The details are details of sacrifice and of watching the Holy Spirit cause skills and ability to grow. We are getting a picture of the integration of work and worship and of grace and action all beautifully woven together, detail upon detail. Exodus gives us the closest thing to an ancient documentary film about the workshop of a master.

> *There is no shame in the beauty of work.*
> *The wisdom of the scribe depends on the opportunity of leisure;*
> *and he who has little business may become wise.*
> *So too is every craftsman and master workman*
> *who labors by night as well as by day;*
> *those who cut the signets of seals,*
> *each is diligent in making a great variety;*
> *he sets his heart on painting a lifelike image,*
> *and he is careful to finish his work.*
> *So too is the smith sitting by the anvil,*
> *intent upon his handiwork in iron;*
> *the breath of the fire melts his flesh,*
> *and he wastes away in the heat of the furnace;*
> *he inclines his ear to the sound of the hammer,*
> *and his eyes are on the pattern of the object.*
> *He sets his heart on finishing his handiwork,*
> *and he is careful to complete its decoration.*

So too is the potter sitting at his work
and turning the wheel with his feet;
he is always deeply concerned over his work,
and all his output is by number.
He moulds the clay with his arm
and makes it pliable with his feet;
he sets his heart to finish the glazing,
and he is careful to clean the furnace.
All these rely upon their hands,
and each is skillful in his own work.
Without them a city cannot be established,
and men can neither sojourn nor live there.
Yet they are not sought out for the council of the people,
nor do they attain eminence in the public assembly.
They do not sit in the judge's seat,
nor do they understand the sentence of judgment;
they cannot expound discipline or judgment,
and they are not found using proverbs.
But they keep stable the fabric of the world,
and their prayer is in the practice of their trade.
—The Wisdom of Sirach 38:24, 27-34

One of the recurring themes I find in ministry with creative people is the pervasive guilt they feel for not "having a real job." There seems to be a deep belief that creative work is not really work. Because of this belief, many artists choose to find jobs that do not use their gifts in order to "fit in."

The closest thing in the Bible to the descriptions of Bezalel's labor are the pages and pages of "begats." These are the lists of genealogies that fill chapters of Genesis, Chronicles, and Numbers. Those lists affirm life and tell the story of how God works through families. The descriptions in the last five chapters of Exodus serve a similar purpose. They are affirmations of the life of work.

In the next chapter we will look at the most important work that Bezalel accomplished.

NINE

Bezalel Made the Ark

"And Bezalel made the Ark..."

These are the first words of Exodus 38, and when I read them a year ago my mind began to race. After eight years of education in two of the finest evangelical schools in the United States, I had never read those words. Or maybe I read them, but they didn't register. You see, I was never taught who actually did the work of building the Tabernacle. If you were like me, I thought there was a nameless and faceless army that did the work under the watchful direction of Moses. Since the Ark of the Covenant is an object of mystery, I assumed its origins were just as mysterious as its disappearance.

> *Bezalel made the Ark of acacia wood; two cubits and a half was its length, a cubit and a half its breadth, and a cubit and a half its height. And he overlaid it with pure gold within and without, and made a molding of gold around it. And he cast for it four rings of gold for its four corners, two rings on its one side and two rings on its other side. And he made poles of acacia wood, and overlaid them with gold, and put the poles into the rings on the sides of the Ark, to carry the Ark. And he made a mercy seat of pure gold; two cubits and*

a half was its length, and a cubit and a half its breadth. And he made two cherubim of hammered gold; on the two ends of the mercy seat he made them, one cherub on the one end, and one cherub on the other end; of one piece with the mercy seat he made the cherubim on its two ends. The cherubim spread out their wings above, overshadowing the mercy seat with their wings, with their faces one to another; toward the mercy seat were the faces of the cherubim. —*Exodus 38:1-9, (emphasis mine)*

It should not surprise us that the details of the Ark are as intricate as the details of the curtains. There is enough detail here that a modern craftsman could pretty accurately replicate at least the general form, if not the artistic details, of the Ark.[26]

And along with these details, we find that the other really important objects of the Tabernacle were made by Bezalel. He made the Table of Showbread, and the Altar of Incense. He made the Brazen Altar that we mentioned in the first chapter. And he designed the Menorah, probably the most powerful image in the Jewish imagination. All of it made by his hand, and all of it made of pure gold.

Tribal Pride

As I have mentioned, this detail of Bezalel making the Ark has often been overlooked. Before we examine some reasons for this, let's consider how Bezalel's relationship with the Ark impacts Israel's history.

Remember, Bezalel is clearly a member of the tribe of Judah. Both the Ark and the Tabernacle itself would have a strong connection to Judah, and eventually end up in the territory belonging to Judah. When I "connected the dots" that Bezalel made the Ark, I suddenly began to see some later events in Scripture differently.

---

26   I discussed this with a master craftsman, Murray Hart, and he pointed out that a woodworker would still have problems with this description. There are no indications of how the joints were made, how the wood was joined together, or which direction the poles were attached.

When the Ark was returned to Israel after being captured by the Philistines, the Ark was returned to Beth-Shemesh, a Levite town. The Levites, who should have known how to handle the Ark, looked inside and were killed.[27] As a result the Ark was sent to the town of Kiriath-Jearim and it stayed there for 20 years. Kiriath-Jearim was a town in Judah.[28] Judah's stewardship of the Ark is the first indication of a future shift in the worship of Israel. In that 20 years, a lot of things happened—both Saul and David would become kings in Israel.

When we read the Biblical descriptions of the day David brings the Ark into Jerusalem, and we see him dance with exuberance before the procession in his underclothes, we are watching a man who has a real connection to this object—it was made by one of his forefathers. David had an organic tribal connection to the Ark because of Bezalel. This direct connection to the Ark would be expressed in the worship movement he established in Jerusalem. There would be two places of worship, one with sacrifice, and one with praise. As we noted, Solomon will begin his reign at the place of sacrifice, before the altar made by Bezalel.

Because of this tribal connection the Ark ends up in Jerusalem. It's about family.

Once again you can pull on the threads of this Biblical tapestry, and another thread emerges. This thread is the tension between the tribe of Judah and the tribe of Levi. As the story in I Samuel reveals, the Levites didn't know how to steward holy things. This is a theme throughout the stories of Samuel and David. Eli and his sons in the first chapter of I Samuel are the leaders of a religious mafia run by the tribe of Levi. And this detail would continue right up until the time of Jesus. The men who led the call to crucify Jesus were Levites, members of the priestly class. The Levites conspired to crucify a member of the tribe of Judah. This tension is in the story of Bezalel.

---

27 I Samuel 6:19.

28 II Chronicles 13:6.

Another Maker

God never discards a person after they have done a service for Him. God honors those who work for him. This may be the greatest contrast between the Kingdom of God and the kingdoms of men. Men use others to build their kingdoms and then they discard the builders, while God always remembers someone who faithfully serves Him. Although we have no record of what happened to Bezalel, or even what happened to the Ark in the end, God has kept a record of the work, and who did it. This little detail about the Ark is what sets Bezalel apart, and also may be why he is forgotten.

In Deuteronomy 10:3 we have a disturbing verse. It is one of the clearest contradictions in the Bible. The book of Deuteronomy is largely composed of the last speech made by Moses before the people cross the Jordan into the Promised Land. Almost everyone who left Egypt with him is dead, Bezalel included. It's Moses' "final word" on all that is recorded in the previous four books.

In Deuteronomy 10 Moses says:

> So I made an Ark of acacia wood, and hewed two tables of stone like the first, and went up the mountain with the two tables in my hand. And he wrote on the tables, as at the first writing, the ten commandments which the LORD had spoken to you on the mountain out of the midst of the fire on the day of the assembly; and the LORD gave them to me. Then I turned and came down from the mountain, and put the tables in the Ark which I had made; and there they are, as the LORD commanded me. —Deuteronomy 10:3-5

If you have been paying attention, you will notice some big problems. First, this description is out of order with the details of the Exodus account. This passage eliminates the two callings of Bezalel, and all the details in Exodus 35-40. According to Exodus, the Ark was constructed after Moses returned from the second time on the mountain. And finally, Moses takes credit for the work—but can't accurately describe how the Ark was made based on the earlier descriptions.

In order to reconcile this, one rabbinic tradition explained that Bezalel was a 13 year old boy who did all the work under the watchful supervision of Moses. Most Christian scholars simply skip this material altogether. Once again, because Bezalel was an artist, and considered a "minor" figure, there seemed to be no reason to explore the issues in the text.

Truth in the Tension

There is an old saying in the Jewish Community, "Wherever there are two Jews, there are three opinions." It is in the tension between points of view that the truth becomes evident. There are many times in the Bible where there seems to be an apparent contradiction, but really there are different perspectives. Remember, the Bible is not a list of precepts or fables with mottoes at the end. The Bible is a living story that in the end reveals the Word made Flesh. The Bible's different perspectives force us to wrestle with truth. It should be no surprise that the Bible eventually reveals that the Truth is a person, not an idea or a set of presuppositions.

Later editors could have "fixed" this contradiction in Deuteronomy, but instead it was left alone. I think this gives even more credibility to the inspiration of Scripture. We are forced to wrestle with the character of Moses, and we are forced to ponder the relationship between Bezalel and Moses.

Leaders and Artists

Moses was a charismatic leader, and I believe that the relationship between Moses and Bezalel may have been tense. Charismatic leaders often struggle when one of their subordinates is more gifted, talented, and anointed than they are. As we mentioned earlier, Bezalel receives a level of gifting that is reserved for God alone in the rest of the Bible. For a leader with any insecurity, that could be a threat.

The picture we get of Moses in Exodus, and especially in Numbers, is of a man "in over his head," trying to single-handedly manage several million former slaves. Things did not run smoothly, and I am confident that he was not the builder of the Ark or the Tabernacle. He was just too busy.[29] Even at the end of his life, Moses reveals a deep insecurity, and lashes out in anger by striking the rock in Numbers 20, as a rebuke to the people. The fact that striking the rock prevents Moses from going into the Promised land indicates this incident was probably a symptom of other problems, not the cause.

God is in the details, and when you study the chapters describing the work of Bezalel you notice a detail that develops as the work nears completion. In Exodus 38 the phrase "as the Lord commanded Moses" appears in the text after each new description. This phrase is repeated continually as the work was finished. I believe this was to reassert Moses' authority over the project, even though Moses was probably not overseeing the activity.

Over the years I have taken on many church commissions for banners, altar decorations or vestments. The hardest commissions have been the ones from churches where I attended. In most cases my work exceeded the expectations of the church or the pastor. This was a double whammy—because the pastor would sometimes feel threatened by my talent. And sometimes, especially in the case of a really successful project, the pastor would take credit for the project.

When Moses goes to see the finished work, his response seems to be surprise. When you compare multiple translations, it seems that Moses has the "aha!" moment that often comes to non-artists when they see a finished work.

> *And Moses saw all the work, and behold, they had done it; as the LORD had commanded, so had they done it. And Moses blessed them.* —Exodus 39:43

Like the experience of many non-artists, Moses sees the work, and "Behold!" It was exactly as the Lord commanded. And Moses blesses them. If Moses had made the Tabernacle, then he would not have been surprised.

From here, the Bezalel story seems to end. And it ends with a detail not mentioned in the text. Bezalel has been the commander of an army of

---

29   Exodus 17:12-27.

artists. He has been filled with the Holy Spirit and been given the ability to do all kinds of crafts. *And now, he completely surrenders his best work to Moses, and releases the Ark and all the Sanctuary furnishings for the Holy Place.*

Bezalel will never see the Ark again.

And Moses, well, later on he will take credit for the work. Deuteronomy 10:3 shines a light into the deep parts of Moses' character that prevented him from entering the Promised Land. It also sheds light on why we have never heard much about Bezalel. The traditions of men will eventually say that Moses oversaw the work with an army of nameless and faceless workers. It sounds harsh, but this is what I was taught in seminary.

Continuing the Tradition

Throughout the writing of this book I struggled with the seemingly hidden tension between Moses and Bezalel. As I have shared this with small groups and various leaders, their reactions were universally negative. Some felt threatened by it, and others felt threatened by me even exploring it. But including it was clearly necessary—and risky— because it might transform your life.

I shared this part of my book with a close friend, Ed Tuttle. Ed is a working designer, and has done a lot of work in and for the church. He immediately identified the relationship of Bezalel and Moses with the struggle he has faced as an artist in the church. The long Judeo-Christian tradition of misusing and abusing artists began at the root. It began with the relationship with Moses and Bezalel.

Maybe you have had a similar experience. Maybe you have been asked to do something for a leader and you exceeded expectations. Maybe you sacrificed personally to see the work completed. Maybe in the end you were overlooked, forgotten, or maybe you weren't paid what you were promised. Maybe you have had the experience where others have taken credit for your work, or you have watched others "eat your lunch," receiving the benefits for the work you did. Maybe another artist or ministry plagiarized (that is, stole) your work, but because they were better known or well connected, they were not held accountable. Maybe you were the ox that was forced to pull the cart of evangelism.

Even if Moses or any other respected leader did something like this, it is not okay. God wants you to know that your work is valuable, and that you as an artist have value. No matter who the leader was, their behavior was wrong. In this new season, leaders no longer have permission to take advantage of "nameless and faceless" people to build their empires. God isn't into empires, God is into the Kingdom.

Experiencing Healing

In order to move on, it might be wise to take some time and forgive anyone who followed Moses' example. Bless them and pray for them, that they would discover their true identity.

When I find myself in a moment like this I say this out loud:

" I forgive _____ for _____." (And be specific.) Then I say to myself "(Use your own name) I forgive you for your sinful reaction to _____."

Finally I release God from any resentment or rage I have by saying "God I forgive you for allowing _____ to hurt me." Although this last statement may sound like bad theology, you would be shocked at how many Christians are angry at God for things that people have done. By forgiving God, you are opening up the channel of grace for healing. After you have forgiven the person who wounded you, ask God to release healing of that wound.[30]

You will be amazed at what happens. Often God will show you a picture of where He was when the wound occurred. I have seen many people get set free and released into new opportunities and blessing after this prayer.

One of the most treasured objects in human history was made by a man filled with the Holy Spirit and given extraordinary gifts. His story

---

30   This model for the healing of memories was taught to me by my confessor, Father Al Durrance in Winter Park, Florida. You can read Father Al's homilies at <u>www. durrance.com</u>

seems to begin and end with sacrifice. And then the story seems to end. But Bezalel's story is not finished, and in order to finish it, we need to look at the larger context of the Ancient world.

TEN

Bezalel the Priest

Many people read the Bible with the idea that it emerged in a vacuum. We forget that there were cultures existing at the same time as Israel, and their impact on ancient Israel was huge.

Bezalel is a prototype for all Kingdom Artists and Culture Shapers. In order to fully understand his role in the Bible and for us today, we also need to look at the role of the artist and artisan in context. Remember, context is everything.

Ancient Mediators

The backdrop for the book of Exodus is the civilization scholars call the Ancient Near East. These are the peoples and cultures that lived in the land that stretched from Egypt to what is today modern Iraq. These were the cultures that Ancient Israel encountered as they traveled, and these were some of the cultures that they attempted to drive from ancient Canaan.

Outside of Ancient Israel, the artisan had a unique role. To a technologically primitive society, a person who could create things seemingly out of nothing was believed to have semi-divine qualities. A person who could take metal and shape it over a forge, or take wood and carve it into the shape of an animal or person (or god) was seen as a person who was making invisible things suddenly visible.

In that world, a person who could do this was perceived as one who had inherently supernatural ability. Because the artisan could seemingly bring things out of heaven, they began to be seen as mediators between the gods and men. As I mentioned in my last book, *An Army Arising*, the meaning of the word "charash" or artisan, shares this understanding:

> *Already we are seeing the principle develop that part of the nature of God is to be an artisan whose work creates a bridge between the spiritual and natural realms. **In the same way, the nature of an artisan is also to create a bridge between the natural and spiritual realms.**[31]*

In the polytheistic, pagan cultures around Israel, there was no boundary preventing the worship of what the artisan created and the worship of the artisan himself. The idol maker had a semi-divine status because he was making objects of worship and those objects were divine. We in the West forget that in the ancient world a statue of a god was the god. Artisans were mediators, or go-betweens between the gods and humanity. "This role as mediator is closely related to the role of the artisan as one who gives form to substance. Similar roles are apparent in the gods of the Ancient Near East."[32]

Bezalel emerges against this larger context, where artists are worshiped or given somewhat priestly status. Given the descriptions of Bezalel in Exodus, he is extraordinary compared to the average artisan of that day. As scholar Max Weber notes, Bezalel is "... credited not only with skill, intelligence, and knowledge, but with having been filled with the Spirit of God, that is, he becomes a charismatic individual of sorts."[33]

---

31   Otto, 14.

32   MacNutt, Paula M. *The Forging of Israel: Iron technology, Symbolism, and Tradition in Ancient Society*, A+C Black, 1990, 228.

33   Weber, Max, *Ancient Judaism*, 1952, 28.

From an "orthodox" perspective, Bezalel is a problem. There already are priests of the tribe of Levi. In the Bible there seems to be a constant struggle with the people adopting the idols and the practices of the surrounding nations. The last thing the people need is a home-grown version of semi-divine priestly idol makers. And the last thing the leaders of Israel wanted was a mediator between God and men outside the framework of the priestly system.

In this context, Bezalel was a priest in the mind of the people. And he was supernaturally gifted beyond those who were officially given the title "priest." And as Israel struggled to be faithful to God, the need to remove any tendency for idol worship became more important. So, as a result, Bezalel, beginning in Deuteronomy 10:3, moves further and further into the shadows.

> *Part of the diminishment of Bezalel was to destroy the chance of a cult around him. "Bezalel in the shadow of God, Son of Light," divinely charged master craftsman of the Tabernacle, might still be liable to veneration.*[34]

By the Greco-Roman period, Bezalel is reduced to a "humanly chosen member of a team of architects."[35] And by the rabbinic period he becomes a thirteen year old boy simply following the instructions of the older Moses.[36] By the time of the Reformers, Bezalel has completely vanished from the imagination.

In the Order of Melchizedek

In some ways Bezalel parallels another person in the Bible, the ancient priest-king Melchizedek. Melchizedek seems to appear out of nowhere, and then once again disappears into the shadows. In the Bible he plays really no role at all until we come to the book of Hebrews:

---

34 Fine, Steven, *Art, History, and the Historiography of Judaism in Roman Antiquity*, (Leiden:Brill) 2014, 36.

35 Fine 2014, 24.

36 Sanhedrin 69b., jewishencyclopedia.com.

For this Melchizedek, king of Salem, priest of the Most High
God, met Abraham returning from the slaughter of the kings
and blessed him; and to him Abraham apportioned a tenth
part of everything. He is first, by translation of his name,
king of righteousness, and then he is also king of Salem, that
is, king of peace. He is without father or mother or geneal-
ogy, and has neither beginning of days nor end of life, but
*resembling the Son of God **he continues a priest for ever**...*
For it is evident that our Lord was descended from Judah,
and in connection with that tribe Moses said nothing about
priests. This becomes even more evident when another priest
arises in the likeness of Melchizedek, who has become a
priest, not according to a legal requirement concerning bodi-
ly descent but by the power of an indestructible life. For it is
witnessed of him, "Thou art a priest for ever, after the order
of Melchizedek." —Hebrews 7:1-4, 12-15 (emphasis mine)

Some of the parallels between Melchizedek and Bezalel include Bezalel's origins, and his disappearance. If you compare the importance of his work with Miriam and Aaron, it's surprising that there is no account of his death. Bezalel, like Melchizedek received an offering out of the spoils of war. Bezalel was not of the tribe of Moses. Bezalel has a name that can be translated to describe his person. All of this causes me to wonder, was Bezalel a priest in the same way that Melchizedek was a priest? I think there is at least the possibility.

Who made the Brazen Serpent?

Over the past year of research, I have had a sense that there is a tension between the tribes of Levi and Judah. I noted this tension in the previous chapter. We see it as we follow the story of the Ark, and if we look at the Tabernacle of David. Simultaneously, there were two competing places of worship run by two different tribes. It has made me wonder if there was a "priesthood" of Bezalel, if only in the imagination of the people.

In Numbers 21:4-9 Moses is instructed to make a "brazen serpent" and put it on a pole. This object heals every person who has been bitten by poisonous snakes. Although the text says Moses made the brazen serpent, evidence suggests Bezalel could have been the one who made it. As we noted earlier, Bezalel is the only person in the Old Testament described with the gifts of sculpture, metal working, and casting. This sculpture becomes an object of healing, but later on, it becomes an idol. King Hezekiah destroys it in II Kings 18:4. A cult had risen around this object, and I wonder if a cult had also arisen around its maker.

Bezalel clearly bears the characteristics of a priestly figure. And as a prototype for us, it is a reminder that artistic people carry a valuable commodity—we have been given the ability to make the unseen visible for others. There is real power in this. In our age of overstimulation, we know the power of images, light, and color to change people's views on reality. Creative people are "priests" in a digital visual culture.

The Judeo-Christian tradition has long had an internal struggle with art and artists. I think this struggle began with Bezalel and Moses. I think it may have continued as a struggle between the tribes of Judah and Levi. The struggle continued into the Christian era with the Iconoclasts, and eventually with the Protestants. As a result, **the people who are the best equipped to meet the needs of this moment in history have been sidelined.**

Throughout the past year and a half I have spent many hours discussing the various aspects of this study of Bezalel, and it is clear that the struggle in the church with the arts is alive and well. Given the shifts in technology and culture, there are many who also feel threatened by the possibility that Bezalel has a larger place in the Biblical story, and that artists may have a much larger role to play than has been traditionally accepted. In the next chapter we are going to look the Messianic aspects of Bezalel as the Bible presents him.

ELEVEN

Bezalel and the Messiah

In the third chapter of the Gospel of John, Jesus says something that is a little startling:

> And as Moses lifted up the serpent in the wilderness, so must the Son of man be lifted up, that whoever believes in him may have eternal life.[37]

I always thought it was a little strange that Jesus makes a connection between himself and a serpent. I thought the connection was even stranger given the fact the Brazen Serpent was considered an idol. The Brazen Serpent is the only historical object Jesus connects to himself in his teaching.[38]

What if this little detail, given the larger context we have studied, indicates that Jesus was aligning himself with Bezalel, who may have been the maker of the Brazen Serpent?

---

37 John 3:14-15.

38 Jesus does refer to several events and miracles from Israel's history including the Manna and Jonah in the Whale as references to himself, but this is the only man-made object he uses as a metaphor in the gospels.

Consider what we have learned about Bezalel:

- Bezalel's name means "shadow" and "Image" of God.
- Bezalel descends from the Tribe of Judah.
- Bezalel's resources come directly out of the first Passover sacrifice.
- Bezalel received an offering from Moses and the people.
- Bezalel is overflowing with the Spirit of God.
- Bezalel is described in ways reserved for God alone.
- Bezalel builds a replica of heaven on earth.
- Bezalel lays down his life and his best work in the construction of the Tabernacle.
- Bezalel acts as a mediator between heaven and earth.
- Bezalel has parallels with Melchizedek.
- Bezalel is eventually despised and rejected.
- Both David and Solomon seem to find a connection with him and his work.
- Philo would later say the name Bezalel means the "Logos of God."

If you know your Bible, the parallels between these characteristics and Jesus are overwhelming:

- Paul says Jesus is the "Image of the Invisible God."
- Jesus descends from the Tribe of Judah.
- Jesus' death and Resurrection happen during the annual Passover sacrifice.
- Jesus is baptized with the Spirit of God.
- Jesus is described in ways reserved for God alone.
- Jesus comes to establish the Kingdom of Heaven on Earth.
- Jesus lays down his life for his "sheep."
- Jesus is the one mediator between God and humanity.
- Jesus is a priest in the order of Melchizedek.
- Jesus is despised and rejected.
- Jesus is a descendant of David and Solomon.
- Jesus is referred to as the "Logos" in the Gospel of John.

Given all these remarkable characteristics, I think we can safely say that Bezalel is a "type" or symbolic representative of Christ. John Gill, the Eighteenth Century Baptist commentator, is one of the few who make this connection:

> *... his name Bezaleel is very significant, and may be rendered, "in the shadow of God"; and he was under the shadow, influence, and protection of the Lord, and was called to be concerned in making those things, which were shadows of good things to come; and he may be considered in all as a type of Christ, who is the chief and master builder of his church, has the care and oversight of it, and under whom others work; for except he built the house, they labour in vain that build it...[39]*

Bezalel is a type of Christ for sure, but is Bezalel more than that? I believe that Bezalel may be a *Christophany*.

Pre-Incarnate Christ

A Christophany is an appearance of Jesus in the Old Testament prior to the Incarnation. In other words, Jesus reveals himself in person. Remember that there are many threads in the tapestry of the Bible, and that the Bible is telling a story. In literature we would call these Christophanies "allusions" to the later story of the Messiah. There are several generally accepted Christophanies in the Old Testament:

- The angel of the Lord who wrestles with Jacob.
- The Fourth Man in the fiery furnace with Shadrach, Meshach and Abednego.
- The angel of the Lord who appears to Gideon.
- Abraham's encounter with Melchizedek.

Given all the evidence, I believe we need to add Bezalel to the list of Christophanies. Given the high level of revelation that Moses received, it makes a lot of sense that Moses would have interacted with the Pre-Incarnate Christ, much like Abraham did when he encountered Melchizedek.

---

39   Gills Commentary on the Old Testament, note on Exodus 31:2, http://www.bible-studytools.com/commentaries/gills-exposition-of-the-bible/.

And if Bezalel is a Christophany, then we need to rethink a lot about what we believe about the Tabernacle, and about the role of the artist in God's economy. And most important of all, if Bezalel is a type of the pre-Incarnate Jesus, then art and artists can no longer be left "outside the camp." They need to be moved to the same location as the Ark in ancient Israel—to the center.

Complete Self-Expression

Think about it. If every element of the Tabernacle speaks of Jesus, of his redemption and our relationship to it, then the maker of it would need a profound revelation of these very things. If Bezalel was Christ in a hidden form, then he was preparing a living parable that would "pre-enact" the saving work he would later do on the cross. All of the sacrifices, festivals, and rituals would act as prophetic preparations for the day when the work would be finished. Bezalel would be activating the power of the cross nearly 1500 years before it happened. More than modern artists who are expressing the deepest parts of themselves in their work, Bezalel is creating an object that is complete self-expression. He and the work cannot be separated. This prefigures Jesus who becomes the ultimate performance artist—God in the flesh. As Paul writes in Colossians: "He is the image of the Invisible God."[40] That word, translated "image," is the Greek word "ikon." Bezalel made the art. Jesus is the art.

A year ago when I began writing this book, I still believed that although the arts were important they were not critical. I believed that art and creativity were only one aspect of the Kingdom of God that needed to be restored, but I was still programmed to believe that artists were always somewhat subordinate to others—like preachers and evangelists.

When I discovered that Bezalel's name meant the "image of God" it was an internal revolution. Maybe my life, and the lives of those who worked with me, mattered more to God than I knew. That initial discovery forced me to keep digging. And as I mentioned earlier, the beauty is in the digging.

Unlike a lot of topics of study, the more I have dug into Bezalel, the more I have uncovered. For Christian artists, we have had few role

---

40   Colossians 1:15

models. It has only been in the last 20 years that many people have paid attention to Bezalel as a possible model for us today. Not only do I think he is our model, I think he is our forerunner. If we are going to enter into the mission of God in the earth, we need to follow the example of this forgotten prophet. If you are an artist or creative person, your prayer needs to be:

God, make me like Bezalel.

In a sense we have jumped ahead and made a conclusion—that through Bezalel there is a Messianic aspect to the arts and creativity. In this sense, there is a unique anointing on the arts for the building and establishing of the Kingdom of God.

At his core, Bezalel embodied the thing he was called to build, a Tabernacle. He was the word made flesh in this sense. Just as he was a prophetic pre-enactor, we are being called like him to follow in this mission.

TWELVE

The Mission of Bezalel

Most Christians know the last words of Jesus recorded in the book of Matthew:

> *"Go therefore and make disciples of all nations, baptizing them in the name of the Father, the Son, and the Holy Spirit."*[41]

This verse has driven many to the ends of the earth, seeking those who have never heard the gospel. For Protestants, the emphasis has often been on the going part, and not necessarily on the "making disciples" part. For some, every other aspect of the Kingdom of God has taken a "back seat" to the mandate to preach the Gospel and baptize.

I hope that this book has challenged you to see a simple fact:

The mission of Bezalel is the mission of Jesus Christ.

Bezalel opens our eyes to a very different image, one of taking territory and making it look like heaven. The language used by one of my favorite preachers is, "Heaven invading earth."

Bezalel's mission is rooted in that first commission of God in

---

41   Matthew 28:19

Genesis—be fruitful, multiply, and subdue the earth. Maybe it will be more clear in less Biblical sounding language: be productive, create, and make the entire earth a place where Jesus can reign as King. The mission of Bezalel is the supernatural use of physical things to create a spiritual inheritance. Maybe Bezalel has been hidden from our eyes for this reason—we weren't ready to see heaven and earth be restored.

Raising up an Army of Bezalels

Bezalel himself was gifted to empower others to help do the work. Even though parts of the Tabernacle were definitely made by him, he raised up others who supported, contributed, and completed the tent of worship. There were others who followed him, maintained the Tabernacle and the Ark, and inherited his spiritual legacy. For the millions of Israelites who didn't have first hand encounters with God, or who could not read the sacred texts, the Tabernacle was their face to face encounter with the God of the Bible, and their experience of the Covenant made with Moses. Just as the great cathedrals of Europe were the Bible of the poor, so the Tabernacle in the wilderness was the Bible to millions. It was a physical witness to the Exodus, and an ongoing prophetic sign of a covenant to come.

The last appearance of the Ark in the Bible is in Revelation.

> *Then God's temple in heaven was opened, and the Ark of his covenant was seen within his temple; and there were flashes of lightning, voices, peals of thunder, an earthquake, and heavy hail. And a great portent appeared in heaven, a woman clothed with the sun, with the moon under her feet, and on her head a crown of twelve stars; she was with child and she cried out in her pangs of birth, in anguish for delivery. And another portent appeared in heaven; behold, a great red dragon, with seven heads and ten horns, and seven diadems upon his heads. His tail swept down a third of the stars of heaven, and cast them to the earth. And the dragon stood before the woman who was about to bear a child, that he might devour her child when she brought it forth; she brought forth a male*

*child, one who is to rule all the nations with a rod of iron,
but her child was caught up to God and to his throne... —
Revelation 11:19-12:5*

Bezalel's Ark becomes a shadow of another Ark, a carrier of a New Covenant not focused on two stone tablets, but on the Living Word. This passage would link Mary and the Ark for centuries in iconography, poetry, and church decoration. But this passage also links the Ark to something else—a cosmic clash of cultures: the culture of Bezalel, and the culture of the Dragon. One would turn earth into a Tabernacle, and the other make the earth a center of commerce driven by lust and uncleanness coupled with power.[42] This last little glimpse of the Ark in Revelation is a window into a culture war that will never end until Christ returns and puts all things into final order.

The role of the artist is ultimately the role of culture shaper. Creativity is not an "extra" in this battle. Creativity is the primary weapon in the arsenal of the army of Bezalels. In another age it may have been fine to ignore God's revelation of himself in the guise of an artist. In this moment, we need to take seriously the mission Bezalel has given to us, and put his life and ministry into the larger context of God's Kingdom in the earth.

Our mission is to take ground, transform space time environments, and provide settings for millions to have face to face encounters with God.

For many years I have worked in and among people who describe themselves as "prophetic artists." These amazing people have been breaking ground in the church. They paint in churches, at conferences, and large worship events. I have been blessed to have these opportunities, and to even have painted before a global television audience. This has been good and necessary, but there is more.

In Times Square in New York City, there are many electronic billboards advertising all kinds of products. When I was a kid these billboards were made of flashing neon lights. Today, because of digital technology, these billboards are living story tellers.

42 Revelation 18.

Imagine a day when a prophetic artist gets the job to design one of these interactive living billboards. Imagine a creative designer with the anointing of Bezalel, a person called and equipped to make an interactive atmosphere of heaven. Imagine a billboard in Times Square, or Piccadilly Circus, or Tokyo, that transforms the reality of that place and causes passersby to encounter the reality of heaven. Imagine another person who designs video games that force gamers to encounter God. Imagine a DJ who mixes house music that delivers ravers from drug addiction. Imagine. Imagine. Imagine.

All things are possible to those who believe.

As this book comes to a close, I hope that it has challenged you, and caused you to rethink all of your assumptions about church, art, and artists. As I have reflected on the details of Bezalel and his life it has caused me to create a "manifesto" based on all I have learned.

THE MISSION OF BEZALEL: A MANIFESTO

1 *Your value is based on who you are and not what you can do.*
Bezalel was not called because of what he could do. He did because he was called. Because his value was in who he was, God didn't forget him. You have value. It's not okay for leaders and ministries to see you for what you can do for them. You are not disposable, you are the Image of God. There is no one else who can do that unique thing you are called to do.

2 *The Call of God makes everything possible.*
Most of what we know about Bezalel came from his call by God. It was a call so important that Exodus repeats it twice. In the call we find out Bezalel's name, his family, and the unique role he is going to play in the history of Israel.

God has been raising up an army of creative men and women across the earth. Whenever there is a new movement of the Holy Spirit, there is the danger to "jump on the bandwagon" and join the trend. Most of the creative people that I meet know that they have a deep call by God to this consecrated life. And then there are those who are well meaning who see the "juice" on the arts today. They want to be where stuff is happening.

Without a clear call from God, you won't have the grace that is necessary to get through the challenges, the criticism, and the real spiritual opposition that comes with the call to transform planet earth.

A few days ago I was talking with my closest accountability partner, and I acknowledged that I didn't have any more options. I could go forward with Jesus and do this "cutting edge" ministry with artists, or I could walk away from the Lord. There was no backup plan. This is what happens to those who are called by God. It's no longer a job or career option, it's your only option. **That narrow focus is the source of your grace and your power.**

3 *Being Like Jesus is not an Option.*
Bezalel was a living parable of the work he was called to do. He became a dwelling place for God so that he could *build* a dwelling place for God.

For most of my life I have witnessed segments of the church giving artists and creative people a "pass" when it came to discipleship. These creatives may have been "cool," but their work was only as deep and mature as their walk with Christ. Some replaced anointing with marketing, and others made money while their personal lives were in deep trouble.

God is calling artists and creative people to shape and change culture. That demands being real disciples of Jesus Christ. It demands knowing your craft, and it demands a commitment to a life of holiness and personal transformation. It means knowing that sexual immorality, gossip, and witchcraft are seen as equals in the New Testament. God wants artists to lead by example, in their lives and in their craft. Purity is about the direction of your life, not sinless perfection. Honestly, I meet many artists who are happy to set up camp in the Wilderness of Sin.

What does this mean? It means walking in healthy relationships with a solid fellowship of believers. It means knowing your Bible, not just a few verses. It means being transformed from the inside out by the Holy Spirit, learning how to recognize God's communication, and discipling others.

4 *Your Source needs to be Supernatural.*
Bezalel experienced God's Provision in an extraordinary way. That provision came in two ways: inward and outward. He was inwardly provided for through the Holy Spirit. The Bible is clear that the Holy Spirit was the source of the 17 creative gifts he walked in. The modern Bezalel has to take the Biblical mandate to walk, live and move in the Holy Spirit seriously. You need every gift and grace God has for you to do this work in a dangerous and hurting world. If you think your natural talent and your clever ideas are enough, think again. All of creation is groaning for the revealing of the children of God to bring something fresh, new, and eternal to a weary world.

I have lived and worked in Salem, Massachusetts for many years. Ironically, the only people I met in Salem who didn't believe in the supernatural were Christians. The modern Bezalel has to reject the ridiculous idea held by many Christians that the Holy Spirit and the gifts stopped working after the New Testament was written. This is not the witness of the first 1000 years of Christianity.

Along with this, our physical and outward needs can be supplied the same way. Bezalel received outward provision through the abundant offering from the night of the first Passover. I don't think there is another artist in history that actually begged for the provision to stop. As the world around us changes, we are going to have to take seriously the need for supernatural supply: finances, transportation, art supplies, connections, opportunities, and a myriad of other needs.

5 *A Creative Life is a Life of Sacrifice.*
Bezalel surrendered the greatest achievements of his life to Moses, and they went into the Tabernacle. Rather than using his gifts to make a name for himself, Bezalel made a place for God. In the end of course, Moses took the credit, and Bezalel was mostly forgotten. Even so, God never forgot Bezalel. His life and his great artistic accomplishments were marked by sacrifice.

From the standpoint of most of the creative community, this sounds like complete nonsense. God is looking for the rare man or woman who is not about establishing their own kingdom, brand, ministry, or line of product. God is looking for that person willing to go low, go underground, and have long term serious influence. It might mean not seeing the fruit in your lifetime. It might mean not having a lot of the perks that many pursue like the newest smart phone, the best clothes, or the most fabulous apartment. It also means that when the perks and prosperity come, and they may because God will bless you, your attitude toward the perks will be very different from those who are driven and motivated by wealth and fame.

6 *The Creative Life is in the Center, not the Fringe.*
There were no words on the Tabernacle. Bezalel communicated using the very best that his age afforded. We are living in a time of technological revolution. Design matters. The look and feel of the "packaging" is as important as the contents. I quoted my friend Rick McKinniss earlier and that line bears repeating. The arts can no longer be the "ox that draws the cart of evangelism." Art and creativity need to be central to the message because the design is the message. The Christian life is bigger than getting people saved—it's about completely renovating the hearts and souls of men and women into little Christs.

Bezalel, that pre-Incarnate Christ, modeled what God wants to do throughout the earth. He took a patch of desert and made a place where people came into direct contact with God. God designed the Tabernacle in detail, and He chose a designer to make it a reality.

7 *The Project God began with the Tabernacle He intends to finish.*
What Bezalel did was just the beginning.

The portable throne built by Bezalel was intended to be a permanent throne. The place where God's mercy is extended is no longer in a tent. It is available to anyone who calls upon the name of the Lord. That army Bezalel taught in Exodus is rising up again. This time instead of changing a patch of desert, this army is rising up to transform culture and create a new humanity.

I live in New England. It is a beautiful place with winding roads, small towns, and little white churches. Most of these churches are empty, and they are monuments to former moves of God and former movements of the human spirit.

God wants to renovate humanity, not make another denomination or revival. God wants to shift and transform civilization. The only way He can do that is through men and women who understand the language of culture and who are empowered by the culture of heaven.

> *God has called you by name and given you a place to belong: and God has filled you with the Spirit of God, with ability and intelligence, with knowledge and all craftsmanship, to devise artistic designs, to work in media, music, and story, in painting pictures, and creating drama, for work in every craft.*

Afterword

In the next book in this series, *Mary: Birthing a Creative Revolution*, we will be jumping forward into the New Testament and looking at how the box Bezalel builds undergoes a transformation. God's throne begins to be built inside human beings.

The adventure is just beginning.

WORKS CITED

Cassuto, Umberto. Piruš ʻal sefer Šemot = *A commentary on the book of Exodus*. Yerušalayim: Magnes, 1953.

Fine, Steven. *Art, History, and the Historiography of Judaism in Roman Antiquity*. 2014.

Fohrman, David, "What does it mean to be Be Tzelem Elokim?" *Ten Minute Parsha video*, AlephBeta Academy, alephbeta.org, 2014.

Justice, Ginny, "The Role of Indulgences in the Building of New Saint Peter's Basilica" (2011). Masters of Liberal Studies Theses, Rollins College, Paper 7.

MacNutt, Paula M. *The Forging of Israel: Iron Technology, Symbolism and Tradition in Ancient Society*. Sheffield: Almond Press, 1990.

Otto, Christ John, *An Army Arising: Why Artists are on the Frontline of the Next Move of God*. Boston: Belonging House Creative, 2014.

Pelikan, Jaroslav, and Walter A. Hansen. *Luther's Works: Lectures on Titus, Philemon and Hebrews Volume 29*. Volume 29. Saint Louis: Concordia Pub, 1968.

Peterson, Eugene H. *The Message: The Bible in Contemporary Language*. Colorado Springs: NavPress, 2002.

Weber, Max, *Ancient Judaism*. Glencoe, IL: Free Press, 1952.

Wolfson, HA., *Philo, Vol. 1*. Cambridge, MA: Harvard University Press, 1948.

Made in the USA
Monee, IL
28 July 2020

37183648R00069